MORE PRAISE FOR
JANET CHEATHAM BELL'S PREVIOUS BOOK,
**FAMOUS BLACK QUOTATIONS**

"Highly prized."
**—Helen E. Baker, Vice President,
Center for Leadership Development**

"There is nothing like a timely, well-placed quote to make one's writing, speaking, or presentations sparkle. And to find that perfect quote there is no more convenient or easy-to-use source than FAMOUS BLACK QUOTATIONS. . . . Highly recommended."
**—*Black Collegian***

"FAMOUS BLACK QUOTATIONS will be useful for a different perspective in the classroom. And students will love its size and price."
**—Edna Pruce, Associate Dean of Student Affairs,
Northeastern University**

"Everywhere I go all over this country, African-American leaders are using FAMOUS BLACK QUOTATIONS."
**—Jeremiah A. Wright, Jr., Pastor,
Trinity United Church of Christ**

"Should have been issued years ago."
**—Gwendolyn Brooks**

*more . . .*

"Fantastic!"
—**Julian Bond**

"FAMOUS BLACK QUOTATIONS is so popular at our stores that it's hard to keep it in stock."
—**Barbara Martin, Manager,**
**Shrine of the Black Madonna Cultural Centers and**
**Bookstores, Detroit, Atlanta, Houston**

"I have been using my very first copy of FAMOUS BLACK QUOTATIONS since it came out in 1986. It is a wonderful collection and extremely useful resource."
—**Deborah Prothrow-Stith, M.D., Assistant Dean,**
**Harvard School of Public Health, author of**
***Deadly Consequences***

"An invaluable reference. . . . The book provides a saying of substance for a variety of occasions. FAMOUS BLACK QUOTATIONS is truly a godsend."
—**Judy Richardson, Blackside, Inc., Education Director**
**and series Associate Producer,** *Eyes on the Prize,*
**Coproducer,** *Malcolm X: Make It Plain*

# VICTORY
## of the SPIRIT

## MEDITATIONS ON
## BLACK QUOTATIONS

### JANET CHEATHAM BELL

**WARNER BOOKS**

A Time Warner Company

Warner Books, Inc., 1271 Avenue of the Americas, New York, NY 10020

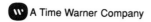 A Time Warner Company

Printed in the United States of America
First Printing: February 1996
10 9 8 7 6 5 4 3

Library of Congress Cataloging-in-Publication Data

Bell, Janet Cheatham.
    Victory of the Spirit : meditations on black quotations / Janet Cheatham Bell.
        p.    cm.
    Includes Index.
    ISBN 0-446-67200-9 (trade)
    1. Black —Quotations.  2. Proverbs, Black—History and criticism.
I. Title.
PN6081.3.B45    1996                            95-39709
081' .08996073—dc20                             CIP

*Book design by H. Roberts*
*Cover design by Julia Kushnirsky*
*Cover illustration, Second Circle Dance, by Phoebe Beasley*

No external force . . . can at long last destroy a people if it does not first win the victory of the spirit against them.

*Howard Thurman*

To my family—
James, Dolores and Reginald Cheatham,
Rosie and Gordon Mickey, Walter Bell,
and in memory of Bonnie Cheatham

For the next generation:
Tony, Kevin, Michael, Gregory and Regina Cheatham,
Miguel, Renee and Madganna Mickey, Kamau Bell

Also, to all the ordinary people who may not have had
wonderfully wise parents who loved them unconditionally.
And especially for those who grew up without hearing that
they could aspire to be whatever they wanted to be.

With all my love and understanding

## Acknowledgments

Among my many blessings is a group of wonderfully support-ive friends/cheerleaders who often have more faith in me than I have in myself. Helen Baker, Mildred Ball, Kainau Bell, Lillian Fleming, Alvin Foster, Paula Grier, Barbara Martin, Carolynn Mazur, Almeda McPherson, Ellen Rolfes, Madeline Scales-Taylor, Jason Smith, Joyce Stricklin, Marcella Taylor, Delores Watson, Arlene Williams, Sani Williams; I am grateful to all of you. A special appreciation is due Ursula McPike and Mary Brennan Miller, both longtime friends and intellectual sparring partners, who were kind enough to read the manuscript and provide essential suggestions that I *be* me in my writing, and to Ellen Gary for our talking walks. Thanks as well to Natalie Fisher and *Unity Magazine* for pointing me in the right direction.

Grateful acknowledgment is made to those who granted per-mission to reprint excerpts from published works.

The excerpt from "Song of Winnie" in the book entitled *Winnie* by Gwendolyn Brooks, copyright © 1991 by Gwendolyn Brooks, published by Third World Press, Chicago, is reprinted by permission of the author.

The excerpt from "The Silver Cell" from the book *I Am A Black Woman* by Mari Evans, published by William Morrow & Co., Inc., 1970, reprinted by permission of the author.

The excerpt from "Incident" by Countee Cullen, from the Countee Cullen Papers, The Amistad Research Center at Tulane University, New Orleans, Louisiana, administered by JJKR Asso-ciates, New York, NY, is reprinted by permission.

The excerpt from "Children Are Not Ours" by Nikki Giovanni is reprinted by permission of the author.

# Contents

# VICTORY *of the* SPIRIT

**Seeking Spiritual Power**

In search of my mother's garden, I found my own.

**Alice Walker**

I began writing *Victory of the Spirit* in an effort to deal with some painful issues—self-doubt, being discouraged, feeling alienated, parenting alone, squabbling with family members, aging—but most particularly trying to pursue my dreams when some of the people who mattered most to me were telling me to give up and get a job.

At age 47, when I quit a "good job" and moved with my 11-year-old son to the city of my choice without first having secured employment, most of my usually supportive family, friends, and acquaintances were appalled. A few people, however, did applaud my courage.

Actually it didn't take courage. I was so emotionally contorted by my effort to fit my creative, free-spirited self into a standard, responsible, socially acceptable lifestyle that I simply couldn't do it anymore. My propelling motivation was the wish to be free of spending most of my waking hours engaged in work designed to maintain a status quo that I found reprehensible. Most of all, though, I wanted to write, whether anybody else thought it was practical or not.

"If I had been able to make the kind of money you make, I never would have stayed with your daddy."

My mother, at age 70, stunned me with those words. I had thought that Mama was "born" to be a wife, mother, and home-maker, and most of the time she promoted that image of herself. There were rare occasions when she spoke longingly of how much she had wanted an education, but most often she extolled the virtues of marriage and motherhood.

After Mama died at age 83, we found several notebooks filled with material she had written about her life. Apparently, she started writing shortly after I was born and continued until a few years before her death.

This is an excerpt from one of Mama's diaries:

I had an urgent desire to go on to higher education. I knew it would be a struggle, but try I would. After being out of [elementary] school a year, I worked as a domestic farm maid, milked six cows twice a day, helped with cooking, cleaning and whatever there was to do around the farm home . . . My salary was $3.00 a week at first, later it was raised to $4.00.

Six weeks courses were given in Nashville, Tennessee, the state's capitol at A and I State College. If one took the course and passed, she would get a chance to teach school and each year continue on from there. . . . I decided to try this. The course cost $25.00, so I started saving my money to attend summer school. . . .

That six weeks will long be remembered. I used a bathtub for the first time, saw movies, rode in a boat and heard some wonderful speeches. It was worth all the hard work and worry of preparing to go.

The following Fall I taught elementary school in Montgomery County at Evergreen School, a one room school with grades from 1 through 8th, about 30 students enrolled, with an attendance of about 20 a day. They lived as far [away] as four miles [and had] to travel on foot . . . My heart went out to them. In rainy, bad weather, sometimes there was only one child [present, the one] who lived where I boarded . . . It has been 39 years since I opened and cleaned that school room that first Monday in September, 1925.

O! how I wanted to further my education in the summer of 1926. Instead of going back to summer school, I came to Indianapolis, hoping to work, attend night school and complete my education that I might be able to help mold fine boys and girls to better the conditions of the world.

Things didn't work out as I'd wished them to. I had no experience other than farm work, which was little or no help in a big city. Factory work, I despised . . . I finally got a job in a private family; stayed on the place . . . It was unheard of for a young girl to take an apartment or room away from relatives. I had nowhere else to go [except to the crowded home of relatives] after I left my room at the private family. I knew I needed to make a home for myself. In view of this, I married on the 16th of June 1927.

After her four children were in school, Mama attended night classes for several years until she received her high school diploma. She was as excited and proud as I can ever remember seeing her.

Because Mama persistently nagged me to "settle down"—to get married and have a family—I had thought that my desire for a career, which was always stronger than any wish to have a husband and children, was an act of rebellion. Now I suspect that Mama influenced me more than I knew and that I'm living the life she wanted to have as an educator and writer. My tribute to her is to live it well.

Over the past ten years my life has evolved into one with which I feel a growing ease. The work I do is meant to empower people by making transformative ideas easily accessible.

More important, I am at peace. I know myself better than I ever thought possible. This self-knowledge is the result of psychotherapy and my continuous contemplation of the eloquent and profound words of those who preceded me on the path of self-examination. More times than I can count, these words have led me to creative insights specific to my own situation.

I have collected some of the quotations that I found most helpful and provocative, and I have written about the ways in which I learned from them. I hope this effort will be useful to others who are seeking their own spiritual power.

## You Have to Get Up

A system of oppression draws much of its strength from the acquiescence of its victims who have accepted the dominant image of themselves and are paralyzed by a sense of helplessness.

**Pauli Murray in *Song in a Weary Throat***

I had to make my own living and my own opportunity. But I made it. That is why I want to say to every Negro . . . don't sit down and wait for the opportunities to come; you have to get up and make them.

**Madame C. J. Walker**

Madame Walker was born on a plantation in 1867, just two years after the Civil War ended; her parents had been enslaved. She married when she was 14, was a mother at 15, and widowed by 18. Despite her background, this African American woman went on to become this country's first female self-made millionaire and a major philanthropist. The obstacles in the way of her achievement were bigger than anything we can even imagine today.

Harriet Tubman and Frederick Douglass were in bondage, legally considered to be the property of others, but they got up, freed themselves, and helped to free others. Tubman, Douglass, and Walker humble me. Thinking about the barriers they faced makes me feel embarrassed to complain about any struggles I have on the brink of the 21st century.

When we reflect on the lives of people like these, what genuine excuse can we offer for not making some effort to improve our lives today?

### What You Can Do

You have to focus on what you *can* do. There are people who convince themselves that they can't do anything with their lives because of what's happened to them—and they're right. They can't. But the reason is that they've told themselves they can't.

**Wally "Famous" Amos**

I am most effective when I approach a task that I believe I'm capable of doing. If I think I can't do something, chances are I won't even try to do it. Of course, if I don't make an effort, I won't accomplish anything. When I do try something, feeling shaky about whether or not I can do it, I quit when I don't reach my goal right away, or the first time somebody reinforces my doubt with skepticism.

Although changing negative thought patterns to positive ones can be simple, I found it to be extremely difficult. After decades of thinking (and being told) that certain challenges were more than I could handle, I needed a lot of time and work to change my expectations of myself. I had to learn to believe that I could do anything I really wanted to do.

Now, when those negative thoughts creep up (and they still do), I force myself to think of the good things in my life. Sometimes I even make a list of my blessings. This causes me to smile, and I start to feel better right away. Once I replace depressing thoughts with more positive ones, I usually receive some material reward, such as an encouraging telephone call, a check in the mail, or a useful new idea. Repeated experiences of this type have led me to believe that negative thinking actually blocks the flow of positive energy.

# Self-Contained

I have
never been contained
except I
made
the prison . . .

**Mari Evans in "The Silver Cell"**

We humans know how to torture ourselves with our imaginations. We do it by having guilty consciences, being ashamed, feeling insecure about our worth, perceiving injury when there is none intended.

I remember an occasion when I was offended because I passed an acquaintance who didn't speak to me. I wondered if she knew I had been talking about her. Later I learned that she was distracted because her child had just been in an accident.

Another time I almost convinced myself not to apply for a publishing fellowship because I imagined that among so many applicants, I wouldn't have a chance. Fortunately, I realized that I couldn't possibly be selected if I didn't apply. I did receive a fellowship and had a marvelously enriching experience that continues to benefit me.

I have hesitated to share a shameful secret with friends because I thought they might judge me, only to discover later that the same problem was an issue for them.

It seems that the simplest and most effective way for me to live is to be honest, straightforward, and loving, of myself and others. That way I won't construct any prisons for myself.

# Make Your Life Work

Can't nothing make your life work if you ain't the architect.

### Terry McMillan in *Disappearing Acts*

Two women I know—one a friend, the other a relative—who had been homemakers both lost their husbands after more than 30 years of marriage but they handled their grief differently.

One widow, grief-stricken, missed her husband so much that she rarely went out. As she became more reclusive, everyone, including her children, found visiting her to be unpleasant. She complained that neither her friends nor her children treated her with the same regard as they had when her husband was alive. Although she never actually looked for work, she insisted that nobody would hire a woman her age.

The other widow decided to take classes so that she wouldn't spend her time thinking about what might have been. Within three years, she had completed the degree toward which she had worked before she married. After graduation she accepted a stimulating and satisfying job, where she made several new friends.

Each of these women faced the same obstacle—the loss of her life partner—and each made a choice. One decided to feel sorry for herself and bemoan her fate. The other chose to be her life's architect and make the new circumstances work for her. Though it isn't always easy, I choose to grow from adversity.

## Doing As I Choose

An artist must be free to choose what he does, certainly, but he must also never be afraid to do what he might choose.

**Langston Hughes**

Never be limited by other people's limited imaginations . . . You can hear other people's wisdom, but you've got to re-evaluate the world for yourself.

**Mae Jemison**

Because I am self-employed and often short of cash, people frequently make suggestions about ways for me to make some "real money." If I'm going to write, they say, I should write a sexy, scandalous book or a mystery novel. Since most people are only impressed by lots of money and fame, they are not easily convinced that doing as I choose is more important to me than either one.

There have been times when I considered taking a job with a regular paycheck, but I've had those before, so I know that increased purchasing power will not satisfy me. Sometimes I get depressed because I don't know where my next dollar is coming from, but that happens less often than it used to, because time and again I've managed to obtain the amount of money I need at just the right time.

The longer I follow my mind and do what satisfies my soul, the more confident I become that my own imagination is as good as anybody else's, and will support me in the life I choose.

# *"I've Changed My Mind"*

It is going to be different now. I'm going to join in the fight wherever [blacks] ask for my help, and I suspect my activities will be on a greater and more intensive scale than in the past.

**Malcolm X**

I admired the late Malcolm X because, despite being a public figure, he had the courage to say that he had changed his mind and would not be doing some things he had done in the past.

One of the most difficult things for me (and most other humans) to do is to change my mind publicly. The worst part is having to say, "I was wrong. I made a mistake." It takes courage to make that admission, especially when you have prided yourself on always knowing what you're doing.

I've learned to admit my errors openly, because to deny them would mean having to persist in doing something I don't enjoy, or even worse, not taking advantage of some wonderful new possibility.

## A Long Active Life

If you ask me the secret to longevity, I would tell you that you have to work at taking care of your health. But a lot of it's attitude. I'm alive out of sheer determination, honey!

**A. Elizabeth Delany in *Having Our Say: The Delany Sisters' First 100 Years***

As we grow older, we should change, not only in the way we look, but in our attitudes, in the way we feel about things. Accepting change brings growth; this is what life is all about. Some people get older without growing, and they do everything they can to disguise the aging process. Betty Friedan, author of *The Fountain of Age,* puts it succinctly: "Men and women who deny their age are not open to change."

Getting through life is like dancing to music that only you hear. When the beat changes, and it always does, you must learn new steps. I believe that it is in learning new steps that life becomes an adventure, becomes fun. You have to find the rhythm and move with it. On some occasions, the music stops abruptly, and improvisation is required.

When you dance to your own music, you get a glorious feeling, because then you can stay on the beat effortlessly.

# Finding Opportunity

Opportunity follows struggle. It follows effort. It follows hard work. It doesn't come before.

**Shelby Steele**

It's better to be prepared for an opportunity and not have one than to have an opportunity and not be prepared.

**Whitney Young**

We talk a lot about being given opportunities, but I've noticed that all the wonderful opportunities I've had in my life have required some effort on my part. I believe the best way to find opportunity is to be looking for it.

Most people have been in situations in which they tried to convince someone to try something, but that person continued to respond with reasons why something couldn't possibly work. Often we talk ourselves out of trying something, because all we can see are the obstacles to our success.

Whenever I slip into enumerating the reasons that I can't do something, I try to catch myself, because I know that this kind of thinking leads to more negative thoughts and drains my energy.

I've learned, instead, to make a list, even if it's a short one, of the reasons that I can succeed. When I read over my list, it generates other positive thoughts and helps me to keep moving forward.

When you are looking for obstacles, you can't find opportunities.

### Blind Luck

In a society that still more often thwarts black ambition than encourages it, black success is rarely accidental or ever a matter of simple blind luck.

**Audrey Edwards and Craig K. Polite**
**in *Children of the Dream***

Each of us has the right and the responsibility to assess the roads which lie ahead.

**Maya Angelou in *Wouldn't Take Nothing***
***for My Journey Now***

When I had fantasies about suddenly having lots of money so that I could buy whatever I wanted, I played the lottery. I didn't win a single dollar. All I did was give the state money in addition to the taxes I pay.

I stopped playing the lottery when I heard on a news report that my chances of winning were 25 million to 1. After giving some thought to my own plans, I decided that the chances of my becoming wealthy by working hard had to be less than that.

Playing the lottery, like hoping for any instant success, is an indicator of impatience or hopelessness. We want success, but we don't want to work for it and wait for it. We may not believe that we have what it takes to create our own success, so we put our hopes and money into blind luck.

I believe that good always comes to those who persevere. Rather than trust the luck of the lottery, I survey what I've already done and prepare for my next productive move. I'm putting my energy, and my money, into something that is far more likely to pay off, and over which I have some control—my own effort.

*Patience*

Waiting is a window opening on many landscapes . . . To walk in the light while darkness invades, envelops, and surrounds is to wait on the Lord. This is to know the renewal of strength. This is to walk and faint not.

**Howard Thurman**
**in *For the Inward Journey***

Perhaps my greatest weakness is a lack of patience. When I buy something new, I use it right away. When I decide to do something, I want to complete it instantly. When I get a good idea, I can barely wait to implement it. My need for immediate action has generated lots of headaches and heartaches for me.

When I slowed down and began meditating, I learned that most of my ideas improved with age. The more time I used to prepare for a project, the better the end product. More than anything else, I learned to plant ideas and wait for them to grow and develop, rather than trying to force things to happen according to my own speeded-up expectations.

Often, I have no notion of what the outcome will be, but I know that if I prepare well and remain patient, I can expect the best.

## *"Wasting Time"*

More and more as we come closer and closer in touch with nature and its teachings are we able to see the Divine.

> George Washington Carver in
> *George Washington Carver In His Own Words*

I have an appointment book. Many of the people I know keep track of their lives this way. We live in a society that encourages frenetic activity. People who live unscheduled, spontaneous lives are seen as either lazy or a little kooky.

Thirty years ago when I visited friends in Jamaica, I realized for the first time the joy of not scheduling every minute of my life. In Jamaica, as in many other parts of the world, a more leisurely pace is their way of life.

In the U.S., we are so committed to keeping busy that we don't take time to smell the roses. Once I decided to live life on my own terms, reflection and meditation became an essential part of my day. Rather than being a "waste of time," it is the space where I solve problems, plan projects, and receive new ideas.

I've found that I do this best outside, sitting in a park or walking along the lake. Considering the beauty and color of a flower or the endurance of a tree refreshes my soul and stimulates my mind. The time I spend doing "nothing" is the most productive part of my life.

### One Thing at a Time

In knowing how to overcome little things, a centimeter at a time, gradually when bigger things come, you're prepared.

Katherine Dunham

It is through the practice of goal-setting that one can compensate for life's shortcomings, whether those shortcomings be real—lack of money, limited schooling, or poor self-image—or imagined.

**Dennis Kimbro and Napoleon Hill in**
*Think and Grow Rich: A Black Choice*

One of the best lessons I've learned is not to overwhelm myself by trying to accomplish something all at once. When I first decided to have my own business, I wanted to be a huge success immediately and, in my haste, I made lots of mistakes. Instead of focusing on what I knew how to do, I spread myself thin trying to perform all manner of tasks I knew nothing about.

Gradually, I figured out that by setting specific short-term goals and concentrating on what I did well, I actually could get something done. Amazingly, when I look back at what I've produced, I see that the small undertakings add up to significant achievements.

Like many others, I had been seduced by the magnificent results of other people's work and decided, "I want to do that!" What I couldn't see was all the preparation and incremental steps that had preceded their visible achievement.

## Passport to the Future

Education is an important element in the struggle . . . to help our children and people rediscover their identity and thereby increase self-respect. Education is our passport to the future.

**Malcolm X**

Once they got a whiff of some real knowledge—knowledge that was relevant to them—they educated themselves far better than any public school could have hoped to do.

**Nathan McCall in** ***Makes Me Wanna Holler***

Although people often think that being educated is the result of attending school or college, Malcolm X and Nathan McCall demonstrated that if you really want to learn, it is possible to educate yourself.

There are many people of accomplishment in our history who educated themselves: Sojourner Truth, Benjamin Banneker, Harriet Tubman, and Frederick Douglass never attended school. Although Malcolm attended school, and McCall, college, they felt that it was the reading they did in prison that helped them to learn who they were as black men and to gain self-respect.

I had earned college degrees, but concluded that my life was not satisfying, so I decided to educate myself further. I read books, talked to knowledgeable people, and listened to tapes to acquire the information I needed to change my life for the better.

You have to decide whether the education you've received, in school or on your own, has produced the way of life that you desire. If you are dissatisfied, things won't get any better unless you do something, for as Malcolm also said, "Tomorrow belongs to the people who prepare for it today."

## Plow Up the Ground

If there is no struggle, there is no progress. Those who profess to favor freedom, and yet deprecate agitation, are people who want crops without plowing up the ground.

**Frederick Douglass**

Douglass's provocative speech is just as important for our lives today as it was when he presented it in 1857. In this speech he exhorted Americans to take action if they wanted to abolish slavery: Without action, nothing could be accomplished.

When we see someone like Michael Jordan, who has achieved astounding success, and wish that we could "be like Mike," what we don't see is the struggle that Jordan went through to attain his skills. Nobody starts out on top. Everybody has to take that first step.

Whether the goal is personal or collective, effort must be expended if a condition is to be changed. A person who claims to want a job but does nothing to increase his/her chances for employment has yet to understand that there is no progress without struggle.

Many of us wish to achieve great things. After expressing the desire, however, we must also do the work necessary to reach the goal. When we do take steps to realize our objectives, and we encounter obstacles, we must keep trying.

Michael Jordan was not selected for his high school basketball team the first time he tried out, but that didn't stop him. Frederick Douglass was born into slavery but his goal was freedom, and he was willing to work until he achieved it.

### Stop Playing It Safe

If you run, you might lose. If you don't run, you're guaranteed to lose.

**Jesse Jackson**

I've never been afraid to fail . . . I think I'm strong enough as a person to accept failure, but I will not accept not trying.

**Michael Jordan**

The fear of taking risks is widespread. Many people are afraid to try something that hasn't been done before by someone they know. Although the axiom "Nothing ventured, nothing gained" has become a cliché, few people actually decide that an unknown gain is worth a known risk. Very rarely do people encourage someone with a new idea to go for it. What people most often share is their fear rather than their support.

Without encouragement, it is far easier just to do whatever is expected of someone of your gender, your age, your color, from your neighborhood. It takes courage, and a lot of it, to try something out of the ordinary, to "go against the grain."

I am proud that I did not allow a lack of others' support, or the failure of my own courage, to consign me to a life of "quiet desperation." I've made many mistakes, but I am blessed to have experienced the excitement and satisfaction of accomplishing something I had long dreamed of doing. Even if I hadn't met my goals, I would still consider myself a success, because I didn't play it safe by not trying.

## *Living Through Your Fear*

I believe . . . that living on the edge, living in and through your fear, is the summit of life, and that people who refuse to take that dare condemn themselves to a life of living death.

### John H. Johnson in *Succeeding Against the Odds*

When I read those words in Johnson's autobiography, I had been gripped by fear for several months. After resigning from a position with a Fortune 100 company, where I earned more than 90 percent of working women do, I started my own business. It thrived for the first few years, and I poured my savings into it. Then things changed, and my revenues dropped precipitously. With my savings gone, I was living from day to day. I attended small business seminars and tried the suggestions I heard there, as well as my own ideas, but nothing worked.

To make bad matters worse, I berated myself for every mistake and for not being able to turn things around. I also felt that I had let down people who believed in me. I was desperately afraid that I would have to give up on my dream.

Even though I was familiar with the story of the obstacles Johnson had overcome, I didn't know that he had experienced the same fear I was feeling. That meant that my experience could be lived through, successfully! Johnson made the effort to live my dreams sound exhilarating. This lifted my spirits, and I began to see my struggle as an adventure and to feel that I was privileged because I dared to live on the summit of life.

## It's a Calamity Not to Dream

It isn't a calamity to die with dreams unfulfilled, but it is certainly a calamity not to dream.

Benjamin E. Mays

If you don't dream, you might as well be dead.

George Foreman

Without glorious dreams of feats to accomplish, goals to meet, and ideals to live for, life becomes an exercise in endurance. If we don't aspire to something, we are merely occupying space and killing time until we die.

We all have joy to bring to the world. Some find their life's work in discovering new technology or caring for those who need assistance, others in entertaining us with laughter or astounding physical feats. Each of us has a niche to fill in this life, and when we find it, it feels right and good and brings us peace and satisfaction.

Sometimes we become so preoccupied with what others are doing with their lives that we don't pay enough attention to our own. More often, though, we become entangled in what we think others expect of us. When we use our energy trying to do what we suppose is expected of us, we become confused about what we expect of ourselves.

Each of us must discover for ourselves what our life's work is; we must find our own personal dreams and let those dreams determine the focus of our lives.

## *Dreaming Big Dreams*

[Success] is about dreaming big dreams, setting specific goals and realizing them . . . Once you're committed, somebody will show up to help you make it happen.

**Darnell Sutton**

Most people go through life with their boat tied up next to the pier. What made me a hero was that I weighed anchor.

**Bill Pinkney**

My son dreams of becoming a stand-up comedian. Although stand-up comedy is one of the more difficult to achieve livelihoods one could choose, he didn't hesitate to share his dream with me. As a matter of fact, he made my day when he told me that he was encouraged to go for it after watching me work toward my own dreams of becoming a writer. On the other hand, he was reluctant to tell some other family members what he had chosen to do. To his surprise, when he did share his dreams and plans, many of them expressed support.

That support, however, is inconsistent. My son has been offered positions in family businesses or given suggestions of other things he could be doing. This makes him uncomfortable because it is an indication to him that his career choice is not being taken seriously.

When he becomes discouraged, I explain that his own commitment and willingness to work are his most important assets. I also tell him that only big dreams pay big dividends, and that he's already a success because he's "weighed anchor."

# Making Discoveries for Yourself

We get closer to God as we get more intimately and understandingly acquainted with the things He has created. I know of nothing more inspiring than that of making discoveries for one's self.

**George Washington Carver**

My mother encouraged me to reach for the stars, but she also told me to keep both feet firmly on the ground. I tried to follow Mama's advice; to be ambitious, but also very cautious, not taking any risks.

As an editor for a major publisher, I had already accomplished more than had ever been expected of me. So why couldn't I be satisfied? Although I dreamed of becoming a successful writer, wasn't the writing I was doing for my job enough? What more did I expect?

Who do I think I am? Do I really believe that I can be like Toni Morrison or Alice Walker? Besides, don't the celebrated and wealthy have some special quality that I don't have?

While working to achieve my own dreams, I discovered that many successful people had been plagued by self-doubt, had made mistakes, had failed at something before achieving their goals. I finally understood that nobody lives a mistake-free life. To reach for the stars, I sometimes had to stand on my toes.

*Your True Guide*

There is something in every one of you that waits and listens for the sound of the genuine in yourself. It is the only true guide you will ever have. And if you cannot hear it, you will all of your life spend your days on the ends of strings that somebody else pulls.

**Howard Thurman**

In the quest to discover who I am and why I am who I am, I have spent many hours listening for the sound of the genuine in myself, and I have finally learned to recognize it when I hear it. It has not been easy; it required a commitment of time and effort. It meant spending hours, days, and even weeks alone. It has been worth it because my life is increasingly my own creation, and the joy I feel is beyond description.

I was among those who found the obvious cases of despair— like alcohol and drug addicts—pitiable. I came to realize that there are many socially acceptable ways of avoiding the genuine in yourself. People can do it through casual relationships, health problems, or long working hours.

I discovered that spending fifteen minutes a day (less than two hours a week) in absolute silence, just listening to myself, was an effective way to find out who I am and what I really want.

The first few times I tried it, I kept thinking of all the things I should be doing. However, with practice and persistence in returning to the silence, I learned to hear myself. Gradually, I have become a human *being* rather than a human *doing*.

*Know Your Beauty*

She does not know
Her beauty
She thinks her brown body
Has no glory.

**Waring Cuney in "No Images"**

When I was growing up, my mother was clear about the fact that she did not approve of the way I looked. I was not tall and slim, as she had been in her youth. Following my mother's lead, my older brother teased that because of my size, I'd never be able to get a boyfriend. Despite the fact that this opinion was limited to certain members of my family, I still look in the mirror and see only defects.

The current taste in beauty—very thin women with narrow hips yet big breasts—has not always been the preference in this country and is definitely not the choice in other parts of the world. In real life, the rarely occurring in nature, fashion model crossed with nursing mother, does not appeal to everyone.

Too many women don't realize their own beauty and do everything they can to change their physical appearance in the belief that this will improve their lives, but life-changing improvements must begin on the inside, not the outside. We all know someone who defies all the prevailing standards of physical beauty, yet who is exceptionally appealing—the title character in the movie *E.T.* for example.

Yes, beauty is in the eye of the beholder, but the first person who must behold your beauty is you. Anybody who feels beautiful, is. I am training myself to see my own beauty.

## Personal Power

> If you believe you have power, that gives you power, and if you use it, act on it, you can make things happen.
>
> **Maxine Waters**

There are no people so favored by circumstances of birth, intellect, wealth, or fame that they do not encounter trouble of one kind or another. The difference is not in whether or not we have problems, but in how we respond to the problems we have.

Everybody has personal power and can choose how to use it. It's not unusual to be depressed when you come up against what seems to be an insurmountable obstacle. This has certainly happened to me. However, depression can lead to self-pity, which can destroy you if it lasts long enough.

To stop feeling sorry for myself, I watch funny movies, go to a comedy club, or call a friend who unfailingly makes me laugh. If that fails, I listen to my collection of Motown's greatest hits. No way can I be depressed while listening to that raucous upbeat music. A change in my mood gives me the energy to make a determined effort to overcome the obstacle, no matter how long it takes or how difficult it proves to be.

All of us have the power to provide for ourselves—emotionally, materially—whatever it is that we perceive as essential for our survival.

*The Courage of Your Own Convictions*

I made up my mind not to move.

**Rosa Parks**

If Rosa Parks had taken a poll before she sat down in the bus in Montgomery, she'd still be standing.

**Mary Frances Berry**

Many people lose the courage of their convictions in the face of so-called authorities. Rosa Parks knew how the authorities would respond to her refusal to give up her seat for a white passenger; she had done it before. What she didn't know, at that point, was that the black community would respond with a bus boycott that would change the course of history. Rosa Parks sat there anyway, because she knew the authorities were wrong. She had the courage to defy them.

My siblings and I are fortunate that our parents taught us to have the courage of our convictions. They did this by allowing us to express ourselves freely at a time when the prevailing mode was "Children are to be seen and not heard." They also listened to our side when we had disagreements with other authority figures.

With this kind of support, we all learned to stand our ground and not to be intimidated by a person in a position of power.

### Where Is the Power?

Where is the power? not on the outside, but within . . . Thoughts
are things. You are the thinker that thinks the thoughts, that makes
the thing. If you don't like it, then change your thoughts. Make it
what you want it to be.

**Johnnie Colemon**

What an exhilarating, liberating feeling I had when I first
understood that everything, from the majestic pyramids to the
book you hold in your hands, begins with an idea, a thought.
That means that if I can create something in my mind, I can create it in my life. Before people do anything, they have to think
about it and make the decision to take action.

Even routine activities must be thought about before they
become habitual. For example, a child learning to walk, or an
adult walking again after an accident, thinks about each step. A
person accustomed to walking thinks only of the destination.

Anyone who can think about something as simple as what
clothes she's going to wear to a special event, creating a mental
picture of how she'll look, can also plan and visualize the attainment of other goals. In this way, daydreaming about things we
want to do can affect what happens to us.

Perhaps we underestimate the activity of our minds because it
has always been there, or because we can't look at and touch
our thoughts. We should remember, however, that some of the
things that exercise the most power in our lives—love, hope,
courage, fear—also cannot be seen or touched. We must learn to
rely more on our ability to shape our thoughts.

## Why Is This Happening to Me?

You have to assess every situation that you're in and you have to decide, is this happening because I'm black? Is this happening because I'm a woman? Or is this happening because this is how it happens?

Charlayne Hunter-Gault

It is a need of the spirit not to forget whoever has let you feel beautiful and safe. But the past is not the next amazing possibility.

**June Jordan**

Many years ago, when I was assigned the task of conducting workshops to help educators eliminate biases against females in their teaching materials and methods, I came face to face with sexism. I was startled that professional males who wouldn't consider saying hateful things about blacks to my face were caustic in their condemnation of females. Before that experience I had good reason to believe that most of the obstacles I encountered were a result of racial prejudice.

In the all-black elementary school I attended, the female teachers encouraged me to maximize my skills. In the less supportive environment of my work life, the people in charge had always been white. I hadn't thought much about the fact that they were also usually male.

My experience with the male educators taught me that not only did I have to think about people who had something against blacks, but I also should consider that they might be sexist as well. What a load!

The stress of being on the lookout for both racism and sexism interferes with too many amazing possibilities, so I've decided to approach the world as if there are no people with prejudices. If people act rude or evil, I choose to assume they're having a bad day, or a bad life, and refuse to let them ruin mine.

# Hero Worship

As long as sports provide the only visible, high-status, occupational role model for the masses of black male youths, black superiority over whites [in sports] shall go unchallenged.

**Harry Edwards**

Perhaps the reason some people can become so involved in the lives and exploits of athletes and other celebrities is that they don't believe they can have comparable success in their own lives. Sports columnist Rick Telander, in discussing the disappointment of fans because Michael Jordan didn't live up to their expectations, described it this way: "He wins; we all win. How dare he make our lives ordinary?"

It's sometimes called "hero worship." I think the problem is that the emphasis is on "worship." It seems reasonable to admire and even respect the intelligence, skills, and abilities of athletes, entertainers, and other celebrities, but to get so caught up in their success and failures that it causes emotional devastation is foolish at best. No one else's activities should divert you from paying attention to your own development.

I believe that all of us have the capacity to be our own heroes, to make our own lives extraordinary, if we just put that energy to use for ourselves.

## Two Warring Ideals

One ever feels his two-ness—an American, a Negro; two souls, two thoughts, two unreconciled strivings; two warring ideals in one dark body, whose dogged strength alone keeps it from being torn asunder.

**W.E.B. Du Bois in *The Souls of Black Folk***

When I discover who I am, I'll be free.

**Ralph Ellison in *Invisible Man***

Life was simpler when I was growing up; everything was a matter of black or white. Although we lived in an "integrated" neighborhood, we had very little contact with white people. Schools, churches, and movie theaters were segregated by law and custom, and our family doctor, dentist, and lawyer were all black. We passed white children on our way to school (they on one side of the street and we on the other). We shouted epithets to one another and sometimes had fistfights. Although we black children fought one another, there was no question that we would unite when confronting the real enemy.

My life is more complex now. I work with white people and have very close friends who are white. I've discovered that my white friends and I have more things in common than I would have imagined. I no longer see all white people as the enemy. However, I know lots of black people who continue to see everything in terms of black and white, and they, too, are my friends.

The only way out of this dilemma is for me to continue my search for the person inside my color and the circumstances of my birth. Once I find her, I'll be free of the conflict.

### Paying Attention

Every experience has a lesson . . . You give things power over yourself, and then they own you.

**Wally "Famous" Amos**

I am religious if it means being aware of my life. I know I can't go on singing and performing forever.

**Pearl Bailey in *Hurry Up America and Spit***

If we pay attention to what we see and experience, we will grow wiser with age. But not everyone is paying attention.

Our initial response to everything is internal: first emotional, then intellectual. After we process an event internally, our emotions may cause us to have a physical reaction: laughter, tears, hitting something (or even someone), speaking out, or yelling.

On the other hand, fear of the experience, or fear of the way we feel about it, can cause us to make an intellectual decision to repress any expression of our feelings and to deny that we've even been affected by it. If our feelings are repressed, we can pretend that whatever happened had no impact on us, that it didn't matter. When we decide that it is of no consequence, we have given our power to fear. Fear can stop us from paying attention or taking action to resolve the situation. We miss an opportunity to learn something, to grow.

*Anger*

Rage doesn't need reason. It only needs targets.

**Clarence Page**

A loud voice is not always angry; a soft voice not always to be dismissed; and a well-placed silence can be the indisputable last word.

**Gloria Naylor**

When we become angry, it's difficult not to lash out, to hurt the person who made us mad. I've noticed, however, that when I am really angry, it's often because I've been caught doing something I'd prefer to keep secret. Or, somebody has discovered an aspect of my personality of which I feel ashamed.

In these situations, the quickest way to defend myself is by attacking the other person, and that's most easily done in an attitude of outraged anger. It is usually counterproductive for people to shout at each other in anger, however, because nobody is listening. If, instead of attacking, I examine myself to determine why I'm so upset, I calm down, even though the process can be unnerving. Once I compose myself, I can approach the situation more reasonably and get better results.

For example, when bill collectors were calling me (and some of them were decidedly unpleasant), I wasn't really angry at them; I was feeling guilty because I didn't have the money to pay my debts. Understanding why I felt the way I did often enabled me to work out arrangements favorable to both of us. In any case, I spared myself considerable anguish by looking directly at the actual problem.

# A Long Life

In all my plans and dreaming, I do not remember ever thinking of a long life . . . That neglect to worry about my old age was peculiar . . . [but] due to no laziness or neglect. I was eager to work and work continuously.

**W.E.B. Du Bois** in
*The Autobiography of W.E.B. Du Bois*

What's the point in living to be a hundred if you don't do anything?

**Sonny Rollins**

Like Du Bois, I have no plans for my old age. At age 58 I am more excited about my life than I have ever been. When I was 47 I quit a job that had great benefits, and some people, out of concern for me, asked what I proposed to retire on. My response is that I've already retired from working for other people, and I manage quite happily to go on living and working.

There are people who believe that at a certain age our bodies begin to fall apart. Fortunately, my expectations are different. My mother did not believe in being sick and had only one serious illness, from which she died at age 83. My father's mother (who was born in 1880, when life expectancy for black women was about 40 years) was never ill. She died in her sleep at age 80.

I plan to live a long vital life. In anticipation of this, I quit smoking, and I eat nutritious foods, exercise, and laugh often.

Living a happy and productive life, of course, is far more important than the number of years one is alive. I believe the secret to aging well is an expectation that life will continue to be good and a willingness to embrace change as an integral part of life.

# *Don't Wait for a Chance; Take a Chance*

We cannot stand still; we cannot permit ourselves simply to be victims.

**W.E.B. Du Bois**

For some people suffering seems to be their raison d'être. No matter how many good things they have, they focus on what they don't have, on how unfairly the world treats them. If they also happen to be members of an oppressed group, that gives them another reason to complain. Their constant lament is that "these white folks won't give a black person a chance."

I met a young black man who was vice president of a major corporation at a time when that was even more rare than it is now. When I asked him how he had managed that feat at such an early age, he responded, "I refuse to be a victim." He had held a position with similar responsibilities at another company, but when they refused to promote him, he moved on. He knew his worth and would not allow anyone to devalue him.

We must believe in ourselves enough to stop waiting for somebody to give us a chance. We have to take a chance.

*Words, the Mark of Freedom*

How much of man's destiny turns on the magic of words! . . .
Words—words—words—the mark of man's freedom.

**Howard Thurman in *The Greatest of These***

When I understood how we program ourselves with words, both in expression and in thought, I became very careful about what I said. For example, I had often found myself saying to my son that we were poor. (Something I frequently heard from my mother.) Instead, I corrected myself and told the truth: that I didn't want to spend money on the thing he wanted, or that I would make the purchase later when I had more money.

When I stopped conditioning myself to have a poverty perspective, I began to comprehend that there's more to prosperity than money. I am prosperous because I have friends, family, health, and a livelihood I enjoy immensely. Thinking of myself as affluent means expecting to have the things I want as well as those I need. Consequently, I look for ways to make my expectations real.

Words can make us feel better, or worse. Words can move people to give up their lives or give them hope to go on living. The most influential things in our lives can be captured only in words; can be felt, but not touched: Hope. Fear. Love. Anger. Joy. Despair. Freedom.

## Minding Your Own Business

I cannot give you a sense of the importance of your life. I can confirm it, . . . but I cannot make it so for you. That you must do for yourself. . . . It takes a lot of courage to leave other people alone.

**Anne Wortham**

I have often been moved to tell other people what they should be doing with their lives. Sometimes I have even become frustrated and unhappy when my advice was ignored. Even when my insistent maneuvering to change people's behavior against their wishes succeeded, they resented me, and the relationships were therefore damaged.

My more mature observation is that the most influential persons are those whose lives are a demonstration of happiness, serenity, and prosperity. When I see someone who behaves in a way that I admire, that's the person whom I want to emulate.

I may influence, inspire, or encourage others, but the only person I can control is myself.

# War of Images

The Constitution they devised was defective from the start, requiring several amendments, a civil war and momentous social transformation to attain the system of respect for individual freedoms and human rights we hold as fundamental today.

**Thurgood Marshall**

Presently in America a war is being fought . . . At stake is the way to control the way people think or not think, act or be passive . . . In this war, it's gonna come down to the artist. What is he/she trying to teach us?

**Spike Lee in *By Any Means Necessary:***
***The Trials and Tribulations of the Making of* Malcolm X**

African Americans, while recognizing that no amount of education, money, or hard work has qualified us for full equality as citizens, continue to insist that America must live up to its expressed ideals. Our fight began with the rebellions of those held in slavery, led to legal battles by the NAACP, and grew into the protest marches of the 1960s. We are now engaged in the war of images that Spike Lee describes.

In mass media of every type—television, movies, newspapers, magazines, books—images of African Americans are disseminated. These images are often biased, distorted, and destructive, designed to influence not only how we are perceived, but also how we behave. It is up to us, however, not to be swayed by negative definitions of who we are.

Each of us is at liberty to decide what type of person we are and which words and images convey our best self-perceptions. We can, and should, support and reinforce positive definitions and act to counter those words and images that promote our destruction.

## Critics

Somebody's telling you how to coach when you've been coaching for twenty-two years, and the most athletic thing they've done is jump to a conclusion.

**George Raveling**

Critics always like to pigeonhole everybody, put you in a certain place in their heads so they can get to you. They don't like a lot of changing because that makes them have to work to understand what you're doing.

**Miles Davis in *Miles: The Autobiography***

I recognize that newspaper and magazine columnists and critics have a job that requires them to be as provocative as possible in order to keep their readers interested. I've read so many inept reviews of movies, books, and plays that feature African American experiences, however, that I can only conclude that many critics know nothing about the subject matter and don't find it important enough to research.

Sometimes the criticism is so ludicrous that I want to laugh; at the same time, I realize that many people will read what is written and assume that it is a correct assessment. Apparently, some critics' knowledge of African American lives comes primarily from the images of crime and poverty on the nightly news, yet these critics feel competent to make judgments about the quality of portrayals of black experiences.

It reminds me of a European teacher I had once who preferred *Manchild in the Promised Land* by Claude Brown to James Baldwin's novel *Go Tell It On the Mountain,* because it included "more authentic" portraits of black life. I couldn't convince him otherwise. I've learned to listen only to trusted friends or make my own judgments about what to watch or read.

## Nurturing Our Children

We must nurture our children with confidence. They can't make it if they are constantly told that they won't.

**George Clements**

There is no future in any job, the future is in you.

**Dennis Kimbro and Napoleon Hill in**
*Think and Grow Rich: A Black Choice*

Too many people, in this society that is driven by money and material gain, discourage others from attempting careers in the arts, from becoming, for example, performers, writers, painters, sculptors, playwrights, poets. In my family the children who tended to spend time alone being creative, reading, or quietly thinking, were branded "lazy." As young adults, the "lazy" children expressed interest in one or the other of the arts. Unfailingly, they were told to find something more "practical" to do; something with which they could earn a living.

In effect, this response is tantamount to telling the young person that even though thousands of other people have successful careers as artists, they aren't capable of doing so.

I refuse to take that position with any person—young or not. Instead I tell people to do what they really want to do. There's no point in spending your life doing something that you hate just to have money to buy things. Achieving anything takes hard work, so if you're not afraid of the work, go for it!

The future is in you.

## Changing Family Relationships

Each of us whom my mother had loved withdrew into a numbing frigid sense of disbelief. From the vantage point of sorrow we were unable, unwilling to reach out to each other and confirm the reason for our grief. This lethal silence was more terrifying than the death that inspired it. Family ties, connections were cut.

### Marita Golden in *Migrations of the Heart*

One of the most difficult passages in my life was watching my mother age and become infirm. She, who was strong in her opinions and unswerving in her religious faith, became fragile and wavering. My tall, strong mother needed to be helped on steps and could no longer see well. Mama literally shrank. She had always been several inches taller than I, but the time came when I could actually look down on her.

The woman to whom I had always turned for help and comfort needed my assistance. Making the situation even more complex was the fact that she adamantly refused to acknowledge that she couldn't continue to go it alone. It wasn't easy to provide the assistance she needed while respecting her dignity, and I'm not sure we pulled it off.

Her life was devoted to her family and her death initiated an apparently irrevocable change in our family relationships. My siblings and I are barely able to face one another anymore, possibly because whenever we gathered before, Mama was always there.

I am, perhaps, even more fiercely independent than my mother was, but if the time comes when I need daily living assistance, I hope I remember to accept it graciously.

# Generation Gap

We must transform the minds of Black people by freeing them from . . . their unconscious acceptance of the white man's declaration of Black inferiority.

### Albert B. Cleage, Jr., in *Black Christian Nationalism*

Twenty-five years ago, when I had my first college teaching job, my mother timidly asked me if I was allowed to teach white as well as black students. I was amused by her question until I saw her relief when I said yes. Mama's question was based on the school "desegregation" of a few years before that had allowed black students to attend school with whites, but had not allowed black teachers in the same schools.

With good reason, my mother expected discrimination in every encounter with white people. I see racism in many more places than my son does, but I do my best not to pass my perceptions on to him. On many occasions when my son tells me that he intends to do something, I have to stop myself from issuing a warning. When I have been rejected in previous attempts or know that other blacks have had problems trying that very thing, I want to save him the expected agony.

He, on the other hand, doesn't expect rejection, and when it happens, he doesn't take it personally, because he's sure of who he is.

We have made some progress.

## Finding Fault

Faults are like a hill: You stand on top of your own and talk about those of other people.

**Hausa Proverb**

Very often what most distresses us about other people is something that we privately fear is a characteristic of our own.

The person who perceives herself/himself as having a weight problem notices "overweight" people everywhere. The child who internalized admonitions about being "too light" or "too dark" becomes the color-conscious adult. The person who fears aging is ever alert to signs of advancing age in others. People who don't think much of themselves usually can't see admirable qualities in anyone else.

When I find myself disturbed by someone else's apparent faults, I stop and think: Of what in my own life does this remind me? Then I put that energy to more productive use by trying to reduce the size of my hill.

 *Negative Energy*

Not everybody is healthy enough to have a front-row seat in your life.

**Susan L. Taylor** in *In the Spirit*

A bitter person is a person in the process of destroying himself.

**Dempsey Travis**

A woman whom I have known most of my life and with whom I once had a close friendship is now apparently stuck in a negative energy field. Whenever I talk to her, she complains incessantly about the way she is treated by her husband, her children, her professional colleagues, her friends. At other times, she interrogates me about the details of my life, sometimes expressing sympathy for something I haven't regarded even as disturbing, let alone tragic. She passes her version of my life on to people we both know and frequently interprets our conversation in a way that creates bad feelings all around. She is such a negative force that after talking with her, I'm out of sorts for hours, sometimes even getting a headache.

I have continued to have contact with this woman because we've known each other for so long and shared so much, but after considering Susan Taylor's observation, I am giving myself permission to love this woman from a distance. She may destroy herself with her insistent bitterness, but I'm not going down with her.

 *Positive Energy*

All that you touch,
You Change.

All that you Change,
Changes you.

### Octavia E. Butler in *Parable of the Sower*

I met an astonishing young woman nearly 20 years ago. Although we had similar backgrounds and at the time shared almost the same circumstances, she was much happier than I. She expected people to be kind and friendly; and they were, to her. I had a different experience with the same people.

We were living in an area notorious for its racism, and both needed to move out of dismal high rises. I decided that the safest thing to do was to buy a house in a neighborhood where other blacks lived. She wanted to live in a two-family house in the suburbs near her job. Although I was smart enough not to say so, I thought she was crazy and that she would never find this ideal arrangement. Of course, she found exactly what she wanted.

When she described the type of man she'd like to marry, again I thought she was fantasizing, but she actually met such a man and married him. They've been happy together for more than a decade.

This woman and I have become close friends, and I'm learning to be more like her: to approach life positively, expecting good things to happen.

### True Friends

No person is your friend who demands your silence, or denies your right to grow.

**Alice Walker in *In Search of Our Mothers' Gardens***

If I don't say anything when something causes me either physical or emotional pain, others can easily assume that I enjoy the situation. When I do speak out, and someone tells me that I must keep quiet, then I know that this person does not really care about my best interests. A true friend wants me to be happy and fulfilled, not silently suffering.

Nor would a real friend deny me the opportunity to be all that I can be. When I describe my dreams and talk about moving forward, my friends encourage and support me. The fearful person who wants me to accept his or her own fears is holding me back, not helping me. I prefer to live my life based on what is, not on "what if . . .".

When I find myself interacting with anyone—friend, employer, family member—who discourages my growth and development, I change that relationship. The person who interferes with the realization of my dreams is just as harmful to me as someone who tries to abuse me physically.

### Survivors, Not Victims

We are survivors, not victims, and we have to take a stand . . .
that allows us to move from being the victim of other people's
decisions to the architect of our own well-being.

**Lani Guinier**

Speak softly and sweetly because you never know when you have
to swallow your words.

**Trinidad and Tobago Folk Saying**

I know we're not to say anything at all if we have nothing
good to say. When I feel I must say something that isn't good, I
try to say it as constructively as possible. If I speak while I am
angry or hurt, I blow off steam, but don't accomplish much else.
However, if I think about why I am upset and determine that I
am justified in speaking out, I do so.

Figuring out if the offense is legitimate, or if I'm responding
to the memory of a past hurt, is most difficult. For example, I've
had the experience of breaking the employment barrier against
people of African descent. On two different jobs I was told by
another white employee that I was hired "only" because I was
black.

The first time it happened, I considered cursing the person
out because this galling, insensitive remark reminded me of epithets of which I had been the recipient many times before. I
decided not to be a victim of somebody else's decision to be
narrow-minded, though, and responded instead, "Well, if that's
the reason they hired me, they certainly lucked out, because I'm
also good."

Not long afterward, that coworker was asked at a social occasion what he thought of me as a prospect to take on a major
project. He responded that I would be the perfect person,
because I was very good at my job.

*The Power of Hope*

As long as hope remains and meaning is preserved, the possibility of overcoming oppression stays alive.

**Cornel West in *Race Matters***

I leave you hope . . . A new Negro . . . will benefit from more than 330 years of ceaseless striving and struggle. Theirs will be a better world.

**Mary McLeod Bethune**

An active ingredient in the steady forward movement of African Americans has been our vision that our lives can get better. This hope of advancement and the willingness to work to make it so has allowed us not only to survive, but to flourish. My life is an improvement over that of my parents, just as they were able to achieve more than my grandparents could.

The most lethal aspect of oppression is the excision of hope in the oppressed. Hope is the opposite of despair. People who have no hope that conditions will improve can easily slide into self-pity, which is a prelude to self-destruction.

People who hope to succeed, prepare to do so.

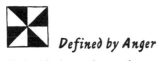

### Defined by Anger

To be black is to live with anger as the defining emotion of a racial experience . . . What all achieving blacks successfully do is turn the color of black into the color of victory.

> **Audrey Edwards and Craig K. Polite in**
> *Children of the Dream*

When I was younger, I felt that if I didn't aggressively look out for myself, I would certainly be taken advantage of. This smoldering anger probably originated when I was not allowed to attend school with the girl who had been my lifelong playmate. Betty and I were born one day apart, lived on the same block, and spent every possible moment with each other. We eagerly looked forward to attending first grade together.

Betty was enrolled in the school down the street with the beautiful green lawn. With the other black children in the area, I walked about a mile past Betty's school to a smaller, drearier building with a gravel playground. A few years later, the schools in Indianapolis were desegregated, and we watched in outrage as the school we had attended was completely refurbished before it was deemed fit to admit white students.

These childhood experiences began the slow boil of anger that moved me as, a young woman, to be ever on the alert for injustices. Of course, the more I looked, the more I found. When I began my search for a more peaceful self, I learned that I could let go of the anger if I altered the way I looked at things. By perceiving myself with my own loving eyes, I stopped feeling the rage. Now, because I am rarely angry, I can see the love other people have to offer.

*America Is Violence Is America*

We make a serious mistake if we try to separate gang and drug violence from the overall violent context of American life . . . Gang [members] and drug dealers . . . have learned the violence-embracing lessons taught in many of our homes and glorified in our mass media only too well.

**Deborah Prothrow-Stith in *Deadly Consequences***

War will stop when we no longer praise it, or give it any attention at all. Peace will come wherever it is sincerely invited. Love will overflow every sanctuary given it.

**Alice Walker in *Living by the Word***

The American Medical Association announced that the U.S. is the most violent nation in the industrialized world, in a report that included all types of violence, not just the violence of the streets.

Our elected leaders decry violence, yet they support the spread of deadly weapons; they say they believe in the sanctity of life, but they promote the death penalty. As long as our law-makers welcome violence by their behavior, their rhetoric becomes simply an indicator of their hypocrisy. They can't lead where they don't go.

Personally, I have decided to make an effort to be more peaceful and loving and to speak out against violence at every opportunity. I also vow not to vote for anyone who promotes and condones violence and my choice will be made based on the candidates' behavior, not on their speeches.

## The Other Cheek

I learned not so much to turn the other cheek as to present, wherever possible, no cheek at all . . . I learned in moments of humiliation to walk away with what was left of my dignity, rather than lose it all in an explosion of rage. I learned to raise my eyes to the high moral ground, and to stake my future on it.

**Arthur Ashe in *Days of Grace***

The West is dying of the effects of its compulsive hatred, and its obsessive wish for revenge.

**Allison Davis in *Leadership, Love, and Aggression***

I was one of the many who watched the brave people led by Martin Luther King, Jr., being beaten, kicked, water-hosed, and spit on without lifting a hand to fight back. Thirty-five years ago, I didn't trust myself not to hurt somebody if I participated in a nonviolent demonstration. However, the more violence I observe in the neighborhood, city, and world that I live in, the better I understand where Mahatma Gandhi and King were coming from.

Nelson Mandela has also set the world a marvelous example. No doubt his amicable approach averted the need for revenge by indigenous South Africans that for years to come could have turned that nation into a bloody battleground much like Bosnia.

We absolutely must stop matching "eye for eye," or the violence will become, in the words of King, "a descending spiral ending in destruction for all."

*In Our Own Hands*

People who are victimized may not be responsible for being down,
but they must be responsible for getting up . . . Change has
always been led by those whose spirits were bigger than their
circumstances.

**Jesse Jackson**

Regardless of what white America does or does not do, the destiny
of African Americans is in our own hands.

**Robert Woodson**

When I was in college, I met a young white woman whose
family background was very similar to my own. Her parents
were poor and uneducated, and attending college was as much a
struggle for her as it was for me. The major difference between
us was that she had not been victimized by racism, but she didn't
seem any better off for having been spared that experience. That
puzzled me. I had thought that if I were white, most, if not all,
of my problems would disappear.

Unfortunately, we have maintained a rhetoric in this country
that implies that being white is automatically better than being
black. This is a dangerous fallacy. It lulls some blacks into
believing that they can't have a good life until they become
white, or as much like them as possible. Conversely, when the
consolation of not being black is insufficient reward for lives
that are a daily struggle, whites are lured into blaming "reverse
racism" or "welfare" for their problems.

We may not be able to close the racial divide, but we certainly
can take our lives into our own hands and stop buying into the
notion that white people must change before we can.

 *It's Up to Us*

No one else can retrieve our values and salvage our people better than we can.

**Dorothy I. Height**

It's not incumbent upon the government to raise our boys. . . .
It is up to us to raise our boys . . . We have handed the lives of our children to our children.

**Spencer Holland**

In the days of apartheid, or *de jure* segregation, as it was officially called, African Americans clearly understood that if whatever ailed our communities were to be corrected, we would have to do it ourselves.

During my childhood, both of my parents volunteered in the neighborhood, doing whatever they could to improve conditions for black people. Mama and Daddy were also active in church and in the PTA, being particularly interested in providing activities for young people, because they knew that young energies not directed productively could easily be misdirected.

Although not everyone was so involved, my parents were not unusual; it was considered the thing to do then. Fortunately, that attitude is returning to fashion in some communities. The more of us who decide that it's up to us to make improvements, the faster we will solve our problems.

 **MAD DADS, Inc.**

Black men must . . . shoulder some of the responsibility for developing personal intervention strategies that will better their condition.

**Thomas A. Parham**

If the Ku Klux Klan comes into our community, we want to fight, but the dope dealers walk up and down the street killing our people all the time and we don't do anything. Brothers, let's regain our cities and rescue our children from drugs, gangs and violence.

**John Foster**

I applaud MAD DADS, Inc. (Men Against Destruction Defending Against Drugs and Social Disorder), and other similar community groups, for taking matters into their own hands.

When we were children, on Saturday mornings Daddy took my brothers, and any other boys in the neighborhood who wanted to go, to the Y. (We had a black YMCA because people of African descent were not allowed to join the white Y.) Daddy also raised funds to buy memberships for boys who didn't have the money to purchase their own.

I am happy to see many indications that we are returning to that spirit of self-help.

# Working Adjustments

Culturally it's important to understand who we are so that when
we interact with whites we do not automatically accept others'
values or give up who we are.

**Maxine Waters**

We worked until the job was done or until we couldn't work
anymore. And even when we'd done everything we could, that
didn't mean . . . a damn thing.

**Walter Mosley in *Black Betty***

Possibly one of the most disappointing revelations for African
Americans was the discovery that being clean and soft-spoken,
graduating from the "right" schools, or moving to the suburbs
did not preclude our being discriminated against. No matter
how many adjustments we made to the alien environments in
which we found ourselves, we were still unwelcome. Ellis Cose's
book *The Rage of a Privileged Class* thoroughly describes this dis-
illusionment.

In my own experience in the corporate world, I worked hard
and effectively—the numbers proved that—but I was never
offered a promotion. This was particularly galling when more
recently hired, less competent people were promoted every time
they completed a project. When I was asked to train a white
male to become my supervisor, I knew it was time for me to
leave.

I understood that much of my unpopularity was due to the
fact I consistently introduced the black perspective in professional meetings. This was interpreted by some coworkers as an
indication that I was antiwhite.

I believe that rapprochement between blacks and whites can
be reached in the workplace only when blacks can be themselves, without whites being offended or threatened, and when
blacks are rewarded fairly for their work.

## Passing the Baton

If each of us will do it and spread it around, we can open up some jobs in [the entertainment industry]. Too often we don't pass the baton along.

Bob Jones

One belief that I share with many African Americans is that we have an obligation, once we manage to get past a racial barrier, to do everything we can to ease access for other blacks. That includes notifying people about job openings, steering contracts to black businesses, and making sure that we introduce the black perspective at meetings.

Some blacks are uncomfortable in a posture of "representing the race" because it draws attention to them when they'd prefer to be colorless, to "blend in." I have no illusions about blending. I know that everybody, even small children, sees color differences, and to talk about "color blindness" is a potentially dangerous fallacy.

There are differences in the way groups of people look. What's important is not to assign negative connotations to those differences. As a member of a group that has suffered more than its share of negative connotations, I take advantage of every opportunity to make things easier for other African Americans—to pass the baton.

*A Choice of Weapons*

Americans too often resolve their trivial arguments by shooting one another to death.

**Deborah Prothrow-Stith in *Deadly Consequences***

Of all weapons, love is the most deadly and devastating, and few there be who dare trust their fate in its hands.

**Howard Thurman in *Concerning Disciplines of the Spirit***

As criminals and the emotionally disturbed kill more people, governments follow their lead and reinstate capital punishment. As assault weapons proliferate among gang members and self-styled militia groups, the state says, "Great idea; let's give guns to everybody." This attitude has resulted in many communities' considering or passing laws that will allow people to carry concealed weapons.

Our politicians seldom have been known for taking the high road, but the present uninhibited, slavish imitation of the lowest element in our society is preposterous. Are Americans really so afraid of love and acceptance that they would prefer to follow the lead of thugs, criminals, and the spiritually bereft? Is anybody thinking of consequences?

In tense relationships I've tried replacing anger with acceptance. More often than not it works to restore peace. On those occasions when it doesn't work, at least the hostility ceases to escalate.

### Role Models

We see basketball players and pop singers as possible role models, when nothing could be further, in most cases, from their capacities.

**Arthur Ashe in *Days of Grace***

So my view of whites was . . . they aren't that important.
They were not (aren't) important enough to define who I am.

**Anne Wortham**

Many people were appalled when NBA basketball player Charles Barkley declared that he was not a role model. I applaud his honesty. As Barkley said, he is paid to be a basketball player, nothing more. We should not expect him, or any other entertainer, to set standards of behavior for us or our children. Despite the hype, they are ordinary human beings who sometimes astonish us with their extraordinary talent.

I suspect that this desire for every black celebrity to be a role model is left over from the days when only a few blacks were allowed to have prominent positions. To show themselves worthy of the opportunity, these black "firsts" felt they had to prove that they were "just as good as whites." This meant that they had to be better, even flawless. As a result we, and particularly white folks, have come to expect every black who is in the spotlight to be absolutely perfect. That's not only unfair, it's ridiculous.

If we define ourselves by our own human standards, we won't have unrealistic expectations of every black person who achieves public acclaim.

# The Family Minefield

A family [can be] . . . a primary defense against not being wanted
and not belonging.

### Howard Thurman in *Concerning Disciplines of the Spirit*

Families are like minefields that we walk and dance through . . .
never knowing where or when something or someone is going to
explode.

### Mary Helen Washington in *Memory of Kin*

I didn't experience my family as providing the expected
defense against my not being wanted, and I remember feeling
that I didn't belong to them. My parents were caring and atten-
tive, so I thought I had no reason to feel the way I did. It took
psychotherapy for me to understand that the genesis of my feeling left out was the lack of attention I experienced at age two,
when my mother had twins.

Without any assistance, Mama was then dealing with a 6½
year old, me, and two new babies. Obviously, she had her hands
full. At two I didn't understand any of this, of course, so I felt
left out, alone.

The four of us competed mightily for Mama's attention, and
couldn't stand it when one sibling or another seemed to be getting more than a fair share. Even though we now are all past age
50, we still relate to each other on the basis of our childhood
resentments.

As I work on letting go of these old, unproductive behavior
patterns, I'm learning to accept that being born into the same
family doesn't mean that we are obligated to help each other,
spend time together, or even like one another. On the other
hand, I know that my efforts to understand and accept myself
for who I am have strengthened me and made me more loving
and accepting of my family.

## If You Loathe the Artist, Can You Love the Art?

Can we keep giving our money to Miles Davis so that he can buy a Malibu beach house and terrorize our sisters in it?

**Pearl Cleage in *Mad at Miles:***
***A Black Woman's Guide to Truth***

I love listening to the late Miles Davis play the trumpet. My enjoyment did not diminish after I read his autobiography, in which he discussed, with candor, his less than healthy relationships with women. After reading Cleage's book, however, I found myself wondering if I could continue to take pleasure in the music of a man who obviously had, at best, a patronizing attitude toward women.

I've concluded that I cannot expect perfection from anyone, artists included, and that although some people are more notorious than others, everybody has problems. As humans, we all make mistakes. And just as I have learned not to judge myself so harshly, I am willing to suspend judgment of others, even those who don't always behave the way I think they should.

Besides, I wouldn't want to discourage creative gifts that might be the only light in an otherwise tortured soul.

*The Woman He Needs*

I had spent my life always becoming the woman men I loved needed me to be. Etching my shadow inside the curve of their love.

**Marita Golden in *Migrations of the Heart***

Every black woman in America lives her life somewhere along a
wide curve of ancient and unexpressed angers.

**Audre Lorde in *Sister Outsider***

Whenever I tried to become the woman the man I loved
needed me to be, the curve of anger eventually expressed itself
and obliterated the love curve.

My mother did her job—raising me to be a properly submis-
sive woman; in her words, making the man believe he was in
charge. I tried to follow her advice, but I had limited patience
with pretense and guile, so my resentment built until it explod-
ed. Then the prolonged argument about my "place" lasted until I
decided that life was too short for me to be so unhappy. After
that it was just a matter of time until I left.

My relationships were based on an acceptance of traditional
gender roles, and physical attraction. Once the initial sexual lure
had waned, there was little to keep us interested, because we
hadn't developed a friendship.

At this point, I am primarily interested in becoming the person that I need.

*Friends as Mirrors*

A person is a person through other persons.

**Bantu Proverb**

When I was a child I assumed that everybody in the world thought the same way I did. After all, my friends and I usually saw things the same way. I've learned better, of course, but I am still amazed at how much alike my friends and I are. We've even discovered that our families are similar as well.

When the behavior of one of my close friends disturbs me, I examine myself, because I know that my friends are my mirrors. From my relationships with other people, friends, family, coworkers, I learn more about me.

As precious as my solitude is, I couldn't grow without the reflection of other people.

 **Women**

The world must choose the free woman or the white wraith of the prostitute. Today it wavers between the prostitute and the nun.

**W.E.B. Du Bois in *Darkwater***

[This is] a country that regards its women as its monsters, celebrating wherever possible the predatory coquette and carnivorous mother.

**Toni Cade Bambara in *The Black Woman***

Women have a difficult time trying to live up to the impossibility of being either "pure" or a "slut." The standard that has been set in this society is that men should be sexually experienced while women remain virgins. This creates a climate in which men may be sexually inhibited with "good" women, then seek "prostitutes" in order to have the kind of pleasure they desire. What are women to do when they encounter these uptight men?

If a woman is forward enough to initiate sex, or sexual variation, she risks being labeled "bad." Many "prostitutes," the women who officially sell sex, despise the men who come to them, because they know that what often drives them there is a contempt for women.

Despite the so-called sexual revolution and contemporary fears of sexually transmitted diseases, people still separate the "good" women from the "bad." Until we women can live our lives as free of sexual and gender restrictions as men are, we are not liberated, and neither are they.

## Men

Men are not women, and a man's balance depends on the weight he carries between his legs.

**James Baldwin in *No Name in the Street***

I love black men, but when a man believes that who he is is located between his legs, he's in trouble. On the other hand, if a man thinks that what's between his legs is of no consequence at all, he's in another kind of trouble. I have to agree with Baldwin: It's all about balance.

Sometimes people are surprised to learn that I like men so much, because I've been single most of my life and had my share of problems with the opposite sex, including two divorces. My husbands had traditional expectations of what a wife should be, and that clashed head-on with what I wanted to do. I don't blame them (anymore); I was the one who was out of step with the times.

My love for black men, though, stems primarily from my loving dad, who took great pride in his children. I also have two protective brothers, five fabulous nephews, a magnificent son, and some close friends who are male.

There have been times when I dissed the brothers, but I've learned to appreciate them more, especially the ones who have found their balance.

## Home Training

Who's raising black men in this country? Black women.
So, if black men are not being very conscious of black women,
then it is our fault.

**Bertha Knox Gilkey**

I believe that boys get an idea of how to treat women from
observing their fathers' behavior with their mothers. Boys are
taught what to expect from women by the way they are treated
by their mothers. In too many cases, women spoil their sons,
not even requiring them to pick up their own clothes. Some
women fawn over their husbands and their sons, so these men
expect the same deference from other women.

In my own family, my sister and I were taught to wash, iron,
cook for, and clean up after Daddy and our brothers. True, my
father worked and provided for the family, but I didn't understand why my brothers should be served. I resented this mightily and carried my resentment into marriage; I was determined
not to be a servant to any other man.

My home training was the impetus for my independence, so
in rearing my son, I trained him to respect women as equal
partners.

*Learning Hard Lessons*

> As African Americans, we find that our self-esteem comes under daily and rigorous assault. Many of us overspend to . . . fend off feelings of rejection, anger and depression.
>
> **Glinda Bridgforth**

> Hard times have a way of teaching us lessons that we refuse to learn in good times.
>
> **Clarence Thomas**

Many of the folks who expressed doubt about my decision to try self-employment were people whose opinions mattered to me, so I needed to show them that I had made the right choice. My way of demonstrating my good judgment was to go into debt by opening an office in downtown Chicago and hiring two employees, long before I was ready for such a move.

This effort to boost my self-esteem by impressing others led me to bankruptcy, but it also forced me to make a brutal reassessment of how I was going to spend my life—doing the things I really wanted to do, or creating an impressive image for other people.

I've chosen to express my individual self and to do what most satisfies me. The people who really love me are pleased when I'm happy. Those who are contemptuous of my efforts have a problem of their own that only they can resolve.

## No Man Around the House

The traditional nuclear family form of husband and wife and their children, with the husband in the work force and the wife-mother as full-time homemaker may not have been made in heaven after all. It may be more accurately perceived as a transitory human response to changing technology.

**Andrew Billingsley in *Climbing Jacob's Ladder***

For a long time as a single parent I bought into the prevailing mythology that "good" families have a mother, father, and children. Eventually, I recognized that throughout our history African Americans have produced a long line of eminently competent and successful people who grew up with one parent and were accomplished in a wide range of fields.

When my son questioned me about the dire predictions for his life chances because of our family status, I told him about people like Frederick Douglass, Booker T. Washington, George Washington Carver, W.E.B. Du Bois, Arthur Schomburg, Richard Wright, Langston Hughes, and Malcolm X, all of whom grew up without their fathers. I also point out contemporaries like Maya Angelou, Bo Jackson, and Debi Thomas, who are apparently thriving after growing up with one parent.

Obviously, the more people growing children have to love and support them, the better. The implication that a man in every home will eradicate America's crime and drug epidemics, or will reverse the decline in educational attainment, however, not only inflates the importance of men, it devalues women and their ability to rear emotionally healthy, productive children.

As Dr. Billingsley notes, the shape of families is changing in the postindustrial era. There is no need for any good parent to feel guilty about going it alone.

## A Lonely Place

The thing that makes you exceptional . . . is inevitably that which must also make you lonely.

**Lorraine Hansberry**

It is generally thought that people don't take risks because they dread failure, but sometimes the fear they have of risking comfortable familiarity is a fear of success.

I wanted to be free to achieve unprecedented success by creating my own work; however, for years I doubted that I deserved the kind of happiness and freedom I longed for. I imagined that if I actually achieved the acclaim I desired, my family and friends might be put off by my achievements, or that "too much" might be expected of me.

When people I cared about told me to "leave well enough alone" or to "get a job," it reinforced my apprehension that a change in my status was not welcomed by those I loved. Even though they were usually motivated by a concern for me, I hesitated to move forward without their unwavering encouragement and support.

When I read the words of Lorraine Hansberry, I realized that I was not the first person to experience the loneliness of stepping off the expected path. That knowledge helps to sustain me.

## Liberating Men

The male cannot bear very much humiliation; and he really cannot bear it, it obliterates him.

James Baldwin

It takes a black man who is supremely committed—and confident—to move beyond primal definitions that would reduce his power to the thrust of a penis.

**Audrey Edwards and Craig K. Polite in**
***Children of the Dream***

Despite their alleged power, I've always thought that being a man is more difficult than being a woman. True, men have access to more jobs, but they have less flexibility in living their lives. It's valid for a woman to be a free spirit, write poetry, or dance. A man who makes these choices risks ridicule.

It's one double standard that favors women: Men are under pressure to perform; women can just be.

A man risks ostracism and a loss of credibility if he decides to nurture his children while their mother works outside the home. We women can dress any way we choose and be considered fashionable. Competent women can cry, pout, and be seductive without losing status. Men are just beginning to cry publicly without being perceived as loathsome.

We talk about our stress, to each other or to men (even if they don't respond in kind), or we go to therapy. Many men are terrified to even think that something could bother them. It's not surprising that they look for ways to escape. Unfortunately, too many of them get away from it all by drinking or working themselves to death. Men need to be liberated too.

## Realizing Dreams Is Hard Work

A dream doesn't become reality through magic; it takes sweat, determination and hard work.

**Colin Powell**

It doesn't matter how many times you fall down. What matters is how many times you get up.

**Marian Wright Edelman in *The Measure of Our Success***

In trying to achieve my dream, I got discouraged when it appeared that I'd worked a very long time without making any progress. To alleviate my despair, I made a list of what I had accomplished. Reading over my list, I was reminded that the years spent actively working toward my dream have been an adventure and a continuing series of lessons and small victories. I must savor these accomplishments, no matter how insignificant they may seem.

If I belabor what's not going right, I stop believing in myself, my behavior becomes self-defeating, and I start to think of giving up. On the other hand, every hopeful step I take, even when I make mistakes, moves me closer to the fulfillment of my dreams.

Besides, giving up because the effort is more than I expected is an admission that I am interested only in objectives that are easily achieved.

## *Children Are Not Ours*

Children are not ours
nor we theirs    they are future    we are past

**Nikki Giovanni**

News stories about custody battles between adoptive and biological parents are yet another reminder that children are regarded as the property of adults. People are outraged over court decisions that return children to their birth parents, but when each pair of parents insists upon exclusive rights to the child, a win-lose resolution is inevitable.

My son, who has always been wise beyond his years, pointed out to me that it would be better for the child if the two sets of parents shared custody; that it is cruel for children to be denied access to a parent because an adult made a mistake. This is a lesson I learned in a different situation.

When my son's father and I split up, we created a palpable tension around the child. It would have been easier for all of us if his father and I had understood that children are not possessions to be used as compensation for losses. The more parents children have to love them, the richer their lives can be.

# Knowledge Is the Key

The individual who can do something that the world wants done will, in the end, make his way regardless of his race.

**Booker T. Washington**

Knowledge is the key that unlocks all the doors. It doesn't matter what you look like or where you come from if you have knowledge.

**Benjamin S. Carson, M.D.**

My father was taken out of school in the 4th grade to work in the tobacco fields; my mother obtained her high school diploma after she was married and had four children. Although my parents' formal education was limited, they were intelligent people with lots of mother wit.

Because they were both from the rural south, where access to education was extremely limited, they made it clear that the opportunity to learn was far more important than the circumstances (segregated schools) under which learning occurred. In addition to insisting that we do well in school and learn as much as we could from our teachers, they somehow found books on the history and culture of black people that they read, and encouraged us to read.

My parents were emphatic that we should obtain as much knowledge as possible, because that was the one thing that could never be taken away from us. Knowledge doesn't eradicate racism or other problems of daily life, but knowing who you are and what you are capable of accomplishing certainly makes those problems easier to deal with.

# Rearing Children to Be Successful

A child who is to be successful is not reared exclusively on a bed of down.

**Akan Proverb**

Most parents want their children to have a better life than they had, so they work hard to provide their children with living conditions and an education superior to their own. Sometimes the quest to protect children from having to struggle leads parents to indulge their children by giving them whatever they want, just for the asking.

Children who have been thus indulged come to believe that the desire to have something is tantamount to acquiring it. These children are deeply disappointed, and sometimes unable to cope, when they discover that life away from home requires more effort than they are accustomed to exercising.

Parents are often surprised when young people who have had the best of everything for 18 to 25 years don't seem able to "get it together." Yet, these young people have never had to solve a problem by themselves, never set and met a goal without the parents either telling them what to do, or doing it for them. In order to deal successfully with adult situations, they first must have learned to handle childhood difficulties.

*Aging*

It took me a hundred years to figure out I can't change the world. I can only change [myself]. And, honey, that ain't easy, either.

**A. Elizabeth Delany in *Having Our Say:
The Delany Sisters' First 100 Years***

The fact that I am nearly 60 startles me. The only thing that keeps me from getting depressed is the exciting new career I began when I was 47. In my mid thirties, I realized with a shock that I could no longer talk about the things I was going to do "when I grow up," because I had grown up.

I believe that the reason so many people begin to have failing health in their fifties is that they feel disappointed in their lives at that point. At 50 and beyond, the children are gone, and working people begin to think of retirement. If your job or your children have been your life, not having them anymore can make you sick. I know that when I was trying to remain in a job that I despised so that I would have good retirement benefits, I began to have all kinds of physical problems.

Like most women, I have been taught that much of my self-esteem has to do with being young and attractive, so getting older is traumatic. I don't look the way I did 20 years ago, but 20 years ago I didn't look the way I did when I was 10, either. And, if I live long enough, the way I look will change again. Women are taught to think that no one will like us as we get older, that we'll just be tolerated as "little old ladies."

I've decided to deal with that the same way I dealt with the warning that my kinky hair style would turn people, especially men, off. If people can disregard me just by looking, that saves me the time and effort of having to talk to them to find out they're narrow-minded.

# Work First, or Family?

Your children need your presence more than your presents.

**Jesse Jackson**

Many companies expect employees not only to give them a full day, but to take work home. Workers who come in early or stay later than required are seen as devoted and worthy of being promoted.

The company didn't come first with me. Whenever I consistently failed to complete my tasks during the workday, I reexamined my approach to determine how I could be more efficient.

I knew I had not found my life's career when a supervisor told me that I acted like my job was not the most important thing in my life. (I wasn't acting.) She was disturbed because I stayed home with my child when he was ill. She felt, and she certainly wasn't alone in this, that my employer should take precedence over my family. I was appalled. I can't imagine that it's good business to ask employees to put company profits above the people they love. Nor can I imagine ever again working at such a place.

## The Battle of the Sexes

They clearly believed . . . that racism is harder on males than females, even though many . . . black women worked for low wages in circumstances where they were daily humiliated and mistreated.

**bell hooks** *in Yearning*

There was a myth . . . that black women had better chances at jobs [than black men]. Well, that was because they scrubbed floors.

**Dorothy I. Height**

There is absolutely no doubt in my mind that men and women see the world differently. I suspect this variation in perception is a result of both genes and training. The unfortunate thing about the expression of this difference is that it is often adversarial, and thereby counterproductive, especially for African Americans. We have so many other issues that require our attention; we can't afford to spend time fighting each other.

Perhaps the most ridiculous issue over which black men and women disagree is the question of who suffers the most from racism. Many black men believe that women are less threatening to white males and consequently have an easier time obtaining positions of power. Even if this were true, why would the inequities of racism make us angry with each other?

Does anybody believe that black women should accept blame for the behavior of racists? Who would benefit if black women turned down opportunities that hadn't yet been offered to black men?

We would all be better served if, in the words of Jesse Jackson, we turned to each other rather than on each other.

## *Finding What You Look For*

Anticipate the good so that you may enjoy it.

**Ethiopian Proverb**

If you go inside where . . . the essence of [our] being is, you are not going to find anything to hang your prejudices on.

**Beah Richards**

One of the special joys in my life has been the opportunity to visit other countries.

I find that people are the same everywhere, but their particular experiences make them behave differently. One must go there, must see people in their own environments in order to appreciate them fully. I've noticed that the behavior of people as "foreigners" is not the same as it is at home, no matter where "home" is.

On one trip to Africa, I went with a group, which was not a pleasant experience. Several members of the group behaved in the stereotypical fashion of "ugly Americans," approaching the Africans as less intelligent, inferior beings. A couple of close friends and I left the group so that we could enjoy the trip.

The Euro-American leaders of our group had told us that Africans have a distinct distaste for African Americans, but my friends and I expected them to be as happy to see us as we were to see them. We were not disappointed. Responding in kind to the gracious welcome of the African people, we had a wonderfully unforgettable visit.

*Weekend Blacks*

My mother viewed speaking impeccably proper English as
a strategy in the overall battle for civil rights.

**Bebe Moore Campbell in** *Sweet Summer*

Being black is too emotionally taxing, therefore I will be black
only on weekends and holidays.

**George C. Wolfe in** *The Colored Museum*

I remember being told as a child that certain topics were not
to be mentioned around white people. We thought that white
people didn't like us because we were different from them, so
we did everything possible to hide our differences and to avoid
living down to their negative images. That meant speaking differently than we did at home and not telling how we did our
hair or what kind of music we preferred.

I knew black people who wouldn't wear bright colors, red in
particular, because supposedly whites always thought we wore
loud colors. We didn't dare mention racism and discrimination,
because we knew whites would find that offensive, and above
all, we wanted to be accepted. These taboos were especially
stringent when a black person was hired to work or attend
school where blacks previously had been barred. I found myself
in those situations more than once.

I briefly tried keeping my real self under wraps during the
week, but it was too much trouble, and my customary forth-
rightness would inevitably break out. Many blacks and whites
have found my candor disturbing. Blacks don't want our
"secrets" divulged, and whites don't want to learn that there are
things about blacks that they don't already know.

My philosophy is that I have to be me. Anybody who can't
accept me as I am, can't accept me at all.

## Connected Lives

Our lives connect in typical family ways: holidays, picnics, births, deaths, the joking and teasing . . . The problem was that in order to be the person I thought I wanted to be, I believed I had to seal myself off from you.

### John Edgar Wideman in *Brothers and Keepers*

I have a brother who is nearly five years older than I and a younger brother and sister who are twins. I used to refer to myself as the middle child, implying all that I learned in child development classes about how middle children are neglected; not receiving as much attention as either the first-born or the baby (in my case it was the babies).

I felt left out, so more than anything else I longed to get away from home. I wanted some individual attention, to be special. I kept moving farther and farther away, putting as much distance as possible between myself and my family. It felt good to meet people who had no preconceived notions about me, who didn't know whose daughter or sister I was. I could create my own persona, try things that a middle child wasn't expected to do.

It's been a wonderful life, and now that I am who I wanted to be, I long for the company of my siblings. I hope we can break the seal.

## Marriage: The Wake-Up Call

She regarded love as possessive mating, and romance as the goal of the spirit.

**Toni Morrison in *The Bluest Eye***

I have a strong suspicion . . . that much that passes for constant love is a golded-up moment walking in its sleep.

**Zora Neale Hurston in *Dust Tracks on a Road***

Growing up, I did not dream of a life with marriage and children. I loved books and greatly admired the women I read about who had careers, but it was a very long time before I had the courage of my convictions and stopped succumbing to the notion that I should have a husband.

I married twice, in response to societal pressure, and more specifically, to my mother's urgent entreaties that I spare her the shame of an "old maid" daughter. Not to imply that I was never "in love." I certainly thought I loved each man; one, in particular, was the love of my life. Since I didn't know me, what I mistook for being "in love" was actually the same sort of emotional distortion Morrison describes.

Because my parents had carefully avoided arguing in front of the children, I had no notion that married couples ever disagreed. In books and magazines, the love stories ended with the golden moment of marriage, and the couple "lived happily ever after." In my own marriages, reality set in almost immediately, and I panicked.

With the benefit of hindsight, I have one suggestion for those who are contemplating marriage: Know yourself and love yourself, so that you may create a satisfying partnership that lasts beyond the "golded-up moment."

### You Can Get Up

In every crisis there is a message. Crises are nature's way of forcing change—breaking down old structures, shaking loose negative habits so something new and better can take their place.

**Susan L. Taylor**

When life knocks you down, try to fall on your back because if you can look up, you can get up.

**Les Brown**

A man I've known for years had an intimate relationship with a woman for several months. When she informed him that she no longer wished to continue seeing him, he responded by saying, "Okay, if that's what you want." They didn't discuss the situation, and he said that it didn't matter to him that the relationship had ended.

Being human, he must have feelings of either relief or sadness about the termination of an intimate relationship; however, he chose not to look at what happened, even electing not to ask the woman why she made that decision. His choices preclude his learning anything from the experience. The problem in that relationship will no doubt recur in subsequent relationships.

Encountering obstacles or having conflicts can teach us so much when we want to grow. We can learn from our troubles if we are willing to look at the causes and consequences. Carefully examining what happened may, indeed, be painful, but if we want to "get up," we must first "look up." Looking up means reading words of inspiration, talking to supportive friends or to those who have had similar experiences, praying, meditating, or obtaining professional help.

The only way to find the message in a crisis is to look for it.

*Setting an Example*

What the [small boy] needs to know is that there are men in this world who are like him, black men, African-American men, who read and write and find the whole process of academics something valuable.

**Spencer Holland**

Children have never been very good at listening to their elders, but they have never failed to imitate them.

**James Baldwin**

My son values reading, because when he was growing up, his father and I read to him and read in his presence. He is honest and industrious because he observed family members and friends engaged in lives of integrity and hard work.

It is impossible for me to convince someone else to spend time doing something that I haven't found worthy of my time.

No matter how much we want children to "do as we say, not as we do," they unfailingly imitate our behavior.

*A Playful Spirit*

Black folks release the stress and tensions in their lives through constructive Play . . . That spirit of Play . . . enables you to lift yourself up when things seem down, to laugh, to perhaps joke about something which is very serious.

**bell hooks in *Breaking Bread***

Sometimes I think that we take ourselves much too seriously. Yes, I know as well as anyone that life is difficult, but I also recognize that humor can serve as a barrier to despair. I believe that, along with music, the ability of African Americans to laugh, play, and party has actually been our saving grace.

Some viewers complained that the television situation comedy *The Cosby Show* was superficial because the show didn't deal with racism, drugs, and poverty. I disagree. Most television images of African Americans (then and now) are of crime and poverty. *The Cosby Show* was a breakthrough that presented a more inspiring positive image. There remains a need in mass popular culture for encouraging representations of people of African descent.

People are rarely inspired to transcend their misery by images of despair, or moved to achievement by being berated for their lack of ambition.

## Money, Money, Money

Since when did money become life?

**Lorraine Hansberry in A Raisin in the Sun**

I have often said that life is not about money; however, I spend a lot of time worrying about not having enough of it. In this society, and perhaps around the world, money is the bottom line. Nearly anything is justifiable if you put a high enough price tag on it. Ask people why they did something foolish, harmful, or counterproductive. If they answer that they were paid an impressive amount of money, no further explanation is required.

Money is so important to us that we sometimes use it to compensate for a lack of love, family, and friendship. I once knew a man who was terrified of intimacy. His wife had divorced him and his children avoided him, but he took great pride in the amount of money he made and the cost of his expensive possessions.

At some point I observed that even people who are really wealthy have the same problems as everybody else: They can be overweight or unhappy, or have low self-esteem. They may struggle with relationships and get divorced. They have health problems. Their loved ones die and they die, leaving their money behind.

Money can make life easier, but money is not life.

*Disastrous Relationships*

Women must know themselves before they go out and get into a relationship. They must know from whence they've come—that history of women—otherwise, the relationship will be a disaster.

**Sonia Sanchez**

The bottom line is to ensure survival, and the best way to do that is to use your head. Use your head before your heart uses you.

**Anne Ashmore**

I know women who stay in long-term marriages by suppressing their own feelings and deferring to their husbands. I had envied them their "happy" marriages until we talked and they told me how much they wished they could be like me. Some of them are quite angry, but they don't talk much about it, because that would mean taking a painful look at all those years of self-denial. My mother's anger didn't surface until a few years before she died.

I was always determined to have my own life, so my relationships with men lasted, at most, a few years. I'm sure that the transience of my relationships had as much to do with my not knowing who I was as it did with gender role expectations.

However, relentless optimist that I am, I still look forward to meeting a man with whom I can have a lasting partnership. And, because I've spent years learning who I am, and why I am who I am, I expect to attract a kindred spirit.

### Apathy or Disappointment?

My mind keeps going back to the millions of youngsters whose parents don't have the sort of jobs a kid would find interesting— digging ditches, cleaning offices, hauling garbage—if they have jobs at all. . . . These are our children, too. Who'll take them to work?

**William Raspberry**

When poor people feel they make a difference, they vote. There's no apathy; there's disappointment.

**Dorothy Tillman**

The poor. The underclass. The disadvantaged. We talk a lot about poverty, but it never goes away, or even decreases. In fact I read a news report that said more people were making less money, and that fewer people are making more money. This news report was about the United States of America, not some "underdeveloped" country.

Many politicians make this bad matter worse by focusing on the red herring of race rather than on economic conditions and employment opportunities. Keeping people furious at that group of people who looks different insures that they will not pay attention to government policies that are gutting everybody, except for the very few at the top. Playing to the electorate's fears has the result that only those who believe the hype will vote, and that the majority of eligible voters won't bother to vote because they know better, or because their only choice is the lesser of two evils.

Even I, a dedicated good citizen, have in most cases in recent years used my vote as a matter of protest, instead of happily voting for someone who I thought would work to improve conditions for everybody. It does not feel good to go to the polls out of obligation rather than with enthusiasm.

### Strong Black Woman

When you're a black woman, you seldom get to do what you just want to do; you always do what you have to do.

**Dorothy I. Height**

Like many black women, I was committed to accepting my responsibilities, doing what I had to do, even if it meant self-neglect. At the same time, I tried to present a strong front, to show that no matter what was thrown at me, I could survive it without any visible damage. Repressing my pain and fear was ravaging; although I denied the impact of events on me, my body didn't.

When I read Bernie Siegel's *Love Medicine & Miracles,* I was startled when I saw, "Women whose children die young or who have unhappy love relationships are especially vulnerable to breast or cervical diseases." Not only had I lost my first son, but shortly after my second son was born, I was diagnosed as having cervical cancer. I was also fiercely protective of my second son, an indication that I had not finished grieving the death of the first one.

Now my second son is an adult living on his own. I miss him; however, I have tried to mourn this wrenching change openly so that my body doesn't absorb it in some health-threatening way. As a precaution, a few months after he moved out I went for a complete physical checkup, my first in several years.

To acknowledge and accept my feelings, I first had to admit that I am an ordinary human being, not some perfect super-woman.

*Habit or Happiness?*

Habit is heaven's own redress:
it takes the place of happiness.

**Alexander Pushkin in *Eugene Onegin***

As human beings we develop all kinds of self-destructive habits: smoking, eating and drinking too much, substance abuse. These overindulgences are usually responses to our unhealthy emotional habits: denying our feelings, living with tense relationships, unresolved grief; the list could go on.

My siblings and I developed ways of relating to each other, based on childhood wounds and birth order, that we have continued to the present day. Evidence that those early perceptions have not healed is that we are all attracted to people, as both friends and spouses, whose behavior re-creates within us the familiar feeling of home. Through these relationships and in rearing our children, we keep trying to rectify perceived childhood slights and parental injustices.

Our childhood seems to have permanently determined how we interact. This doesn't make us happy, but we've formed the habit and can't seem to break it. As I learn to understand these patterns, I am empowered to move beyond them.

## Believe in Health

Whatever we believe about ourselves and our ability comes true for us.

**Susan L. Taylor**

The shape of our bodies undergoes several dramatic, though gradual, changes from birth onward, but who we are, our essence, remains the same. When our bodies do not function properly and need healing, the healing occurs from the inside out. A healthy body begins with a healthy spirit. The ability we have to heal ourselves is what brings about miracle cures and spontaneous remissions.

If we choose to think positively, to remember that who we are is not defined by anything or anyone except ourselves, then we will not be perpetual victims of illness. Medical technology, drugs, and nutritious food benefit us only when we choose to be healthy.

A survey of people who have lived beyond 80 years of age, and who are still active and in good health, revealed that the one thing all of these people have in common is an optimistic attitude. These healthy and busy elders all believe that no matter what happens, their lives will continue to be good.

When we choose to be healthy, that choice is made within. As we think and believe, so we are.

## Your Own Way

There will always be those who are ready to speak persuasively
about the utter impossibilities of your achievement . . . Consider
their words, if you must, then proceed to go your own way.
Listen instead to the inner rhythms of the music within your soul.

**Dennis Kimbro and Napoleon Hill in**
***Think and Grow Rich: A Black Choice***

The people who thought I was crazy for quitting my job and
going off on my own were not as hazardous to me as some of
those who encouraged me. I either ignored the naysayers or dug
in my heels to prove them wrong. However, I was susceptible to
what I heard from those who wanted to help me.

One friend urged me to double the inventory of a product I
was ordering because she knew someone who would sell them
all. She and the person she had in mind were unavailable when
the merchandise arrived. I was furious with her, but actually,
there was no one to blame but myself. Despite this woman's
insistence, I knew she had no experience in what I was trying;
yet I took her advice. I was reminded of the title of a book,
*Beware the Naked Man Who Offers You His Shirt;* I felt as though I
had bought the shirt.

I did learn some important things from this encounter. I am
careful not to offer advice in areas that I know nothing about,
and I no longer accept advice from inexperienced people. When
I do talk to experts, I listen, then follow my own rhythm and go
my own way.

## Life Follows Death

May the moon follow the sun and not fail to rise . . .
And may life always follow death.

### *The Husia: Sacred Wisdom of Ancient Egypt*

Perhaps the most difficult and painful of life's many problems
is the death of someone who is dear to you. When a person
who has been a vital part of your life dies, it can feel as though
you are literally coming apart, that you are no longer whole.
Acknowledging the permanence of the loss can be almost
unbearable.

Accepting that you will never again touch that person, never
again hear that person's voice, never again look into that person's face, never again hear that person's counsel, share a secret,
or exchange a glance, can pull anyone into despair, including
those who consider themselves to be strong and unemotional.

The death must be accepted, mourned, then let go. All three
steps are required to move beyond the pain and recover your
balance. If your feelings are not dealt with, the distress can be
manifested in any number of counterproductive ways.

Inability to concentrate, bouts of depression, irritability, compulsive eating, and a variety of health problems can all result
from not mourning a loss. These new problems prolong and
exacerbate your sense of deprivation and inhibit your recov-
ery—the life that should follow death.

# Fathers and Sons

Fathers and sons arrive at that relationship only by claiming that relationship: that is by paying for it. If the relationship of father to son could really be reduced to biology, the whole earth would blaze with the glory of fathers and sons.

**James Baldwin in _The Devil Finds Work_**

I know a man who longs for a relationship with his grown sons but refuses to initiate it. The man complains that his sons never call or visit him, but neither does he call or visit them. He and his sons, like other fathers and sons I've observed, are engaged in a standoff. I suppose holding your ground is the macho thing to do.

It seems to me that the real problem is that many fathers are not involved with their children while the children are growing up. When there has been no intimacy for the first 18 years, it's rather difficult to be close as adults. That difficulty becomes an impossibility when each person refuses to give in.

Unfortunately, men have been trained to think that their only responsibility as fathers is to provide for their children materially. I've talked to men who sincerely believe that because they were "good providers," their children owe them affection. The fact that they never talked to their children, attended a school performance, or shared an event with them seems not to matter. They believe that being a father is simply a matter of biology. Although biology and material support are important to any child, the father-son relationship requires as much effort as any other good relationship.

*Mama and Daddy*

Throughout the social history of black women, children are more important than marriage in determining the woman's domestic role.

**Paula Giddings in *When and Where I Enter***

My mother rarely worked outside the home. Her job, as she saw it, and according to prevailing values, was to be a homemaker and mother. Mama would have preferred a career, but she felt powerless to make that happen, so she put her considerable intelligence and skills into her children. Her children became her reason for being; she prodded, encouraged, inspired, queried, comforted, and hovered over us.

Like many women whose only venue is their children, she was possessive. We were her children. She was our liaison with Daddy. This was made easier by the fact that Daddy worked long hours. When he wasn't working, he was busy with community activities, an involvement that my mother supported.

Daddy was fun. We looked forward to seeing him. He brought us treats and gave us money. Daddy was there when the family spent Sundays, holidays, and vacations together. Daddy was always called on for major problems, but Mama was there to discuss every disappointment and every triumph.

Small wonder, then, that Daddy occupies a happy but distant place in my heart, and Mama is entwined in every cell of my body.

### Getting Over

Those talk shows would take a black man on television back then
only if he grinned, became a clown, like Louis Armstrong did . . .
I loved the way Louis played trumpet, man, but I hated the way
he had to grin in order to get over with some tired white folks.

**Miles Davis in _Miles: The Autobiography_**

I'd rather play a maid than be one.

**Hattie McDaniel**

Having to live in a society that tries to fit everyone who
resembles you into some degrading stereotype makes it extremely difficult to just be yourself without somebody being either
upset or offended.

Like Miles, I love Armstrong's music, but didn't take kindly to
his "grinnin' and skinnin'." However, the more I think about it,
the less I care. If, for his own reasons, Armstrong felt that he
needed to play the clown to make a space for his extraordinary
music, so be it.

Miles was certainly able to get over with a totally different
personality, but he was born 25 years after Satchmo. Even
though changes in the way African Americans are regarded
sometimes are imperceptible, they do occur.

What is more painful about the response to blacks who take
on roles that other blacks consider demeaning is that too often
we revile the person playing the role rather than the people who
create the roles. What we should remember is that entertainers
need to work at (and be paid for) their craft; they can either perform in the roles available to them, or work at something else.
It's a personal choice that shouldn't have to carry the weight of
the entire culture.

## The Damage of Ridicule

An error means a child needs help, not a reprimand or ridicule for doing something wrong.

**Marva Collins**

My mother was so anxious for me to have a life better than hers that she expected perfection from me. She said I was smart enough to make the highest grades in school, and she was openly disappointed if I did any less. Her high expectations boosted my self-esteem, but her disapproval of my shortcomings contributed to my feelings of inadequacy. Mama had definite ideas about how my life should go, and when I seemed not to be on the path she had determined for me, she let me know it in no uncertain terms.

My uncertainty about whether I should please my mother or follow my own mind created years of confusion for me. However, it did convince me to be understanding of the mistakes my child made and to be accepting of how he leads his adult life.

# My Country, but Not My Kind

America . . . insists upon seeing the world in terms of good and bad, the holy and the evil, the high and the low, the white and the black; . . . damning those whom it cannot understand, excluding those who look different, and salves its conscience with a self-draped cloak of righteousness.

**Richard Wright** in *American Hunger*

[Race] locks white people in a morally and ethically indefensible position they must preserve by force . . . The pervasive violence in our society . . . is rooted in the paradigm of race.

**John Edgar Wideman** in *Fatheralong*

During my senior year in college I lived in a rooming house with several young women from other countries, so they referred to me as "the American." I was shocked at being called an American and initially had no idea whom they were talking about.

Like most folks of African descent, I had grown up as an outsider in this country, thinking of myself as a "Negro." "Americans" were the people who didn't have to fight for everything they needed. "Americans" could live wherever they chose, go to any school they liked, get jobs based on their skills.

It has taken a long time for me to accept the idea that, in fact, I am an American. When I travel outside the United States, I often feel more welcome than I do here, but I am recognized and dealt with as an American, even in Africa.

Still, "Lift Every Voice and Sing" has more resonance for me than the "Star Spangled Banner" ever will. Of course, it could just be the songs themselves: "Lift Every Voice and Sing" celebrates hope and harmony; the "Star Spangled Banner," like America, is about violence and war. However, this is my country, so what I don't like about it, I must work to change.

***Black in America***

The country's image of the Negro, which hasn't very much to do with the Negro, has never failed to reflect, with a kind of frightening accuracy, the state of mind of the country.

**James Baldwin**

There are no good times to be black in America, but some times are worse than others.

**David Bradley**

The mean-spiritedness of the Republican politicians elected in the 1994 "revolution" is expressed in the issues on which they ran for office. Appealing to the electorate's basest instincts and worst fears, they asked for votes based on their promises to punish the weakest members of our society—children, the poor, and those disadvantaged by a lack of education and marketable skills—and to reward the most successful. Their race-baiting "hot-button" issues—welfare reform, crime, affirmative action, rap music—keep people preoccupied while they pass laws to benefit the people who finance their multimillion dollar political campaigns.

We've been here before: In 1896, 78 blacks were lynched, and the U.S. Supreme Court legalized segregation in the "separate but equal" verdict in *Plessy vs. Ferguson*. We survived that in addition to many other ordeals and we will outlast these tribulations as well.

Living through difficult times can either strengthen or destroy you. Black people have always become stronger.

*Helping Children to Grow Up*

Your children will try you at every moment. You will not win all of the arguments. Be prepared to lose some of them because if you win all of them your children will never grow up.

**Toni Morrison**

One thing that my siblings and I remember fondly about our parents is that they listened to us, so we felt valued and loved. I do the same with my own child, and, consequently, he is open and honest with me.

Sometimes, I think, parents create problems for themselves. I've observed parents in heated arguments with their children over how the children should dress. After the first time my child objected to wearing something I had purchased for him, he went shopping with me and selected his own clothing.

I also did not invade his privacy. It never occurred to me to open his mail or search his room. I considered my child's person to be as valuable as my own, so I treated him the way I wished to be treated.

As a result, he is comfortable being himself, and he learned not only to make decisions, but to live with the consequences of his judgments.

# Stirring Up Trouble

Rappers . . . have the power to generate thoughts, make people second guess the system . . . And maybe that's what really scares people about rap—not that it has the power to stir up trouble, but that it makes us think about troubles we'd just as soon shove under the table.

**Ice Cube**

I love Farrakhan. People differ with Mr. Farrakhan because they are afraid the minister can control somebody's thinking, just like people in the media control the thinking of people. They feel now they have to compete with somebody for the minds of these people. He makes them uneasy.

**Mike Tyson**

Although I prefer jazz and blues to rap and don't always agree with Minister Louis Farrakhan of the Nation of Islam, like most black people I take pleasure in the fact that both rap musicians and Farrakhan disturb the powers that be.

African Americans are left out of textbooks, largely ignored in the media, unless there is something negative to report, and used by politicians to frighten the electorate. So, when I see the decision-makers being unnerved by something that a black person does, I sit up and take notice.

Rap musicians and Farrakhan attend to a segment of society that many politicians want to starve out or lock up. When our elected leaders take a position that the people who are most in need should get the least assistance, the disaffected people look elsewhere for direction; it would be foolish of them not to.

## Obsessed with the Enemy

The precious quest for black self-esteem is reduced [by some] to immature and cathartic gestures that bespeak an excessive obsession with whites and Jews. There can be no healthy conception of black humanity based on such obsessions.

**Cornel West in *Race Matters***

There are those in the black community who specialize in reviling the generic whole of Jews and whites for the many and varied abuses blacks have suffered. It is satisfying, at least momentarily, to hear those whose power we have learned to fear being soundly castigated, but how useful is it?

It is natural for there to be strong negative feelings among a people who remain in jeopardy in a variety of ways simply because of the color of our skin. However, once we have agreed on the terrible things that have happened to us and how they occurred, then what?

I believe it is more productive to move creatively forward than to remain in a state of perpetual rage.

## Being a Parent

Parents, don't let your children go, don't let them off, but don't you dare let them down.

**Carolyn Vessel**

I could draw a circle on a piece of paper and my mother made me feel like Van Gogh.

**Damon Wayans**

Perhaps the best decision I've ever made was to become a parent. As a parent, I experienced joyful, uninhibited, unconditional love and affection for the first time. What I learned from my child about love, I'm trying to apply elsewhere in my life.

In my effort to be the best possible parent, I try to recall how I felt about my own child-parent relations. When I open my mouth and hear my mother speaking, I stop to consider what impact those words had on me.

I have unfailingly supported my son's interests, no matter what they are. I don't do this out of blind loyalty, but because I trust his judgment about his life. Besides, I'm so busy with my own life that I can't get involved in managing his adult activities.

*Affirmative Action*

People have been sitting on my neck or my head for a century, and when I get a piece of my neck out, they start this reverse discrimination cry.

John Hope Franklin

I have great fear for the moral will of Americans if it takes more than a week to achieve the results.

Michael Harper

In the 1970s, as the result of a new policy in a large urban school system, I was hired by a major educational publisher to work as a textbook editor. The publisher had been in business more than a hundred years, but I was the first person of African descent to edit its literature textbooks.

Textbook publishers first made an effort to comply with the schools' requirements by coloring some of the faces in the textbooks, then by hiring black sales reps. The school system, however, wanted substantive changes that would have an impact on the information presented to the students. As a result of insistent pressure and the educators' buying power, at age 42 I got the opportunity to work in book publishing, something I had wanted to do since I was about 10.

The new policy was called "affirmative action."

Even the most generous affirmative action program asks for no more than a total of 30 percent of jobs/contracts for "minority" groups, including white women; most programs though, request 20 percent or less. That means that 70 percent or more is still the preserve of white males.

Clearly, 70–90 percent is not enough for them. They've always had it all, and that's the way they'll always want it to be. If we wait for them to offer a piece of the pie, we'll never get our fair share.

*Writing Books Instead of Scrubbing Floors*

I'm less concerned with affirmative action promoting diversity than [with it promoting] opportunity.

**Stephen L. Carter**

Bakke is the white minstrel who corks his skin . . . and dances Jim Crow. . . . Pretending he belongs to an oppressed race frees him to preserve the power of the oppressor.

**John Edgar Wideman in** *Fatheralong*

Affirmative action was initially conceived to compensate African Americans for hundreds of years of unpaid labor and the ensuing years of racial discrimination in employment, education, housing, transportation, and other events of our daily lives. Blacks perceived affirmative action as a substitute for the promised 40 acres and two mules that we never received after the Civil War.

Native Americans, robbed of their lands and livelihoods, were due and have received some remuneration. Japanese Americans, another group owed a debt because of their internment during World War II, were given a cash settlement. Each of these groups was victimized by the laws of the land and by official U.S. government policy, so it is reasonable that in the interest of fairness and harmony, the U.S. government should make restitution.

Without the Civil Rights movement and affirmative action, I would possibly be scrubbing floors for a living rather than writing books. Is that the problem with affirmative action?

# The Collective Good?

I cannot accept the definition of collective good as articulated by a privileged minority in society, especially when that minority is in power.

Wole Soyinka

He who starts behind in the great race of life must forever remain behind or run faster than the man in front.

Benjamin E. Mays

Admittedly, affirmative action has been distorted in its implementation and should be reexamined, but to say that 30 years of halfhearted compliance is sufficient to compensate for 370 years of slavery and maltreatment is ludicrous.

Even though, as with most problems in this country, the issue has been given a black face, there is no argument that white women have benefited most from affirmative action. Those in control don't like sharing power with women either; it's just that criticizing women could backfire at election time.

These people, who feel that their power monopoly is being threatened, seem to believe that a less contentious way to maneuver women back into place is by promoting Wonder Bras, four-inch heels, and butt-hugging skirts. However, they know that if they can destroy affirmative action, it will affect women more than it will ethnic minorities.

Most politicians will call for whatever they think is immediately advantageous, but I don't believe that the people of America, male, female, black, and white, will go back to their behavior of the 1950s.

## My Son a Brute?

Black males have long intrigued the Western imagination, whether as gods and kings in much of classical antiquity, or devils and sambos since the high Middle Ages.

**Henry Louis Gates, Jr.**

One of the ways by which men measure their own significance is to be found in the amount of power and energy other men must use in order to crush them or hold them back . . . The persecution becomes a vote of confidence, which becomes, in turn, a source of inspiration, power, and validation.

**Howard Thurman in *Jesus and the Disinherited***

I well knew from experience and from reading black history that white Americans have an unseemly fear of black men. People who are frightened are very dangerous; however, I still wasn't prepared for the pain when my child was perceived as a fearsome black brute.

Nearly every black man I know has been the recipient of cruelty, either from an official or an ordinary citizen. The brutal treatment may come in the form of hostile speech, a savage beating, or being killed outright, like the 10-year-old black boy who was killed by police for stealing a package of cookies. I recall that even my loving father carried an axe handle in his car so he could defend himself, yet not be subject to arrest for possessing a weapon.

In the preface to the exhibit catalog *Black Male*, Gates reported that in 1990, 2,280,000 black boys and men were jailed or imprisoned, while 23,000 earned college degrees, a ratio of 99 to 1. The incarceration/college ratio for white males is six to one.

Fortunately, the men in my family see this persecution as a vote of confidence and a source of inspiration.

## Who We Are

We are a Black Gold Mine. And the key that unlocks the door to these vast riches is the knowledge of who we are.

**Tony Brown**

The best of black culture, as manifested, for example, in jazz or the prophetic black church, refuses to put whites or Jews on a pedestal or in the gutter.

**Cornel West in *Race Matters***

Every person of African descent in America has been affected on some level by racism, but many have spent their energy creating, as West indicates, the best of black culture; growing past the crises, rather than ranting about them.

Africans in America, prohibited the practice of our own religions, blended our intense and emotional rituals with Christianity to develop a new form of worship. We defined ourselves as gifted, visionary musicians and sang about our frustrations in the blues and our hope in spirituals. We took European musical instruments and created jazz.

For years we were denied the opportunity to participate in major-league athletics, but we overcame that as we have many other obstacles to participation in American life. Hurdles remain, but we know what to do and that we must do it. This is the attitude that makes us great. This is who we are.

## The American Dream

America . . . embitters those struggling hardest to believe in it and work within its established systems [and] is seriously undermining any effort to provide would-be hustlers and dope dealers with an attractive alternative to the streets.

**Ellis Cose in *The Rage of a Privileged Class***

There is nothing more dangerous than to build a society with a large segment of people in that society who feel that they have no stake in it; who feel they have nothing to lose.

**Martin Luther King, Jr.**

The American Dream is generally thought of as the opportunity for a better future for those who desire it and are willing to work for it. Immigrants come to the U.S. hoping that their own lives will improve, and with the expectation that their children's lives will be significantly better.

Many Americans of African descent, although not descendants of voluntary immigrants, still expect that hard work and frugality will benefit them as well. However, as Cose documents in his book, attaining the material goods of the dream is not the same as becoming an accepted and integral part of American society.

Street hustlers in the "hood" are contemptuous of the cost of education in both time and money, and of the perpetual stress of racial discrimination that blacks endure to "move up" in American society. They feel they can acquire the same standard of living with less effort. It's a difficult argument to counter, especially if your goal is the acquisition of material goods.

My own efforts to "move up" have more to do with personal development than with seeking the American Dream.

## Punishing Children or Ourselves?

One reason school staffs are ill prepared for children outside of the average expected, or mainstream, experience is that educational reform . . . [is] focused on academic standards and content rather than on child development and relationship issues.

**James Comer, M.D., in *Maggie's American Dream***

We need to stop punishing children because we don't like their parents.

**Marian Wright Edelman in *The Measure of Our Success***

There is much hand-wringing over low test scores and lack of achievement by children in public schools. School superintendents are hired amidst promises to raise scores and are fired for failure to do so, sometimes just a few months later.

The emphasis is not in the right place. As schools are presently set up, children who come from homes where learning is valued do well in school without much assistance. The problem is with those children who haven't come from nurturing homes that encourage learning. This society has to get serious about offering basic education to all children, and must provide additional resources for children who have not grown up in a supportive environment.

This is not a clear-cut issue of racial discrimination. Many school systems, particularly in cities with overwhelming black enrollments, are operated by African Americans; and, of course, white children are also subject to backgrounds that make success in school difficult. We have allowed public schools to become pawns in games of political power, punishing the powerless, who in turn will punish us by disregarding society's rules and laws.

## "Black People Steal"

We're always talking about blacks as a group and whites as individuals.

**John Hope Franklin**

Our sense of self as black people is always under attack in this society, but it's reaffirmed and enhanced at the moment you take a stance.

**Derrick Bell**

As a parent, I've learned as much as I've taught. My young son gave me a lesson in pride that I won't forget. When he was very young I showed him the store security guard who followed us whenever we shopped. I did this to warn him to be careful and so he would know that all black people are suspected of being thieves.

At 14, my son was accused of theft by a young security guard in a record store, tossed out, and told never to shop there again—this despite the fact that he had not set off the exit alarm and the guard found nothing when my son allowed himself to be searched. He was livid with outrage when he told me what had happened.

I was so relieved that he had not been arrested and beaten or killed that I didn't make much of the fact that he had been grievously wronged. I told him I was surprised it hadn't happened before. However, my efforts to rear him with an inviolable sense of his worth had been more effective than I realized; he was adamant that we protest the treatment he had received.

We learned that the security guard's idea of doing his job was to keep all blacks out of the store. After we contacted the owner and informed him of what was going on, he fired the guard. My son felt better, and so did I.

### Advantage, You

From a distance, it's easy to start thinking that white folks run things because they're especially intelligent and hardworking . . . Up close, most white folks, like most people, are mediocre. They've just rigged the system to privilege themselves and disadvantage everyone else.

**Jill Nelson in *Volunteer Slavery***

Some white people are so accustomed to operating at a competitive advantage that when the playing field is level, they feel handicapped.

**Nathan McCall in *Makes Me Wanna Holler***

When I became the first person of African descent to be hired in a division of a large public institution, I expected that the people already there would be exemplars of competence and mental prowess. What I actually found were people of varying abilities and a lot of negative feedback about my own skills. It took a while for me to recognize that much of the behavior I was attributing to racism was, in fact, raw fear of my expertise.

At one point there was much speculation about and lobbying for the vacant position of division director. I had no interest in the job, because the increased responsibility far outweighed the nominal gain in salary. Almost the first order of business for the colleague selected as director was an attempt to fire me. During the contentious discussions, in his fruitless effort to be rid of me, he told me he knew that I had wanted his new job.

I was stunned. An educated white male (the most privileged class in the U.S.) actually felt threatened by a competent black female. I realized I had power I wasn't using.

*Searching for Tradition*

Only white people have been legitimized as makers of American history. Black people have become its instruments.

**Chuck Stone in *Black Political Power in America***

African American writers who feel snubbed [by being left out of Great Books of the Western World] have linked themselves to the wrong classical traditions and should look instead to their own ancestors in Africa.

**Molefi Kete Asante**

The rules on how to effectively oppress people say that the most important task is to control their access to information about themselves. In addition, it's necessary, whenever information about the oppressed group is disseminated, that it undermine all positive aspects of their culture and encourage everyone to see them as defective. That's why it was illegal in the antebellum South for African descendents to learn to read and why white South Africans insisted that black South Africans learn the obscure Afrikaans language, rather than English.

It takes a totally dedicated and determined person to obtain accurate and credible information on Africans and African Americans in the U.S. Despite the popularity of black athletes and entertainers, our history and culture are not routinely taught in most public schools, or in many universities. Small wonder then that African American scholars find themselves allied to the "wrong" tradition; many of them have no knowledge of anything else.

### It's What You Answer To That Matters

Now I was eight and very small,
And he was no whit bigger,
And so I smiled, but he poked out
His tongue and called me, "Nigger."

I saw the whole of Baltimore
From May until December;
Of all the things that happened there
That's all that I remember.

**Countee Cullen in "Incident"**

It's not what you call us, but what we answer to that matters.

**Djuka**

I once worked for a white male supervisor who was unable to have me terminated because I was better prepared and smarter than he was. My experience confirmed my suspicion that white people are not omnipotent, and altered my perception of racism.

I know now that the average white person is just as insecure as the average black person. This means that ordinary whites have no ability to hurt us except through our belief that whites are all-powerful.

There is, in fact, no reason to be upset because a few bigots call us names or decide to dress up in sheets and march through town. These people have no more power than we do. Their only strength comes from us, allowing ourselves to be hurt by their behavior.

## Unseemly Women

For as unseemly as it may appear now-a-days for a woman to preach, it should be remembered that nothing is impossible with God.

> Jarena Lee in *The Life and Religious*
> *Experience of Jarena Lee,* 1836

I hope that we are not witnessing that dawning of a new intellectual orthodoxy in which thoughtful people can no longer debate provocative ideas without denying the country their talents as public servants.

> **Lani Guinier**

Like many presidential nominees who are opposed by some group, Guinier expected to explain her position in the U.S. Senate confirmation hearings. However, less than six weeks after announcing Guinier's nomination for Deputy U.S. Attorney General for Civil Rights, President Clinton withdrew the nomination. Instead of quietly fading away, Guinier held a press conference. She was following in the footsteps of Jarena Lee, one of the many African American women from our past who have insisted upon being heard. Lee had the heretical idea of becoming an AME minister. After challenging the ban on women ministers, she received permission from Bishop Richard Allen to hold prayer meetings in her home. One Sunday morning Lee got up and began speaking in church. Her skill so impressed Bishop Allen that he endorsed her call to preach.

Every time I read about or observe black women who refuse to stay "in their place," I am empowered. From these women—Harriet Tubman, Sojourner Truth, Ida B. Wells-Barnett, Mary Church Terrell, Mary McLeod Bethune, Fannie Lou Hamer, Winnie Mandela, Joycelyn Elders, Lee, Guinier, and many others—I am reminded not to ignore injustice or tolerate oppression. I will not be silent because others don't want me to speak.

## School Desegregation

Education can be one of the most liberating forces in the world, but it can also be one of the most oppressive. Twelve years of segregated schooling teaches you some powerful lessons not featured in textbooks.

**Robert L. Green in *The Urban Challenge—Poverty and Race***

My initial opposition to school desegregation occurred when I was forced to attend a high school with an enrollment of nearly 2,000 that had about 50 black students. I would have preferred the social life my older brother had enjoyed at the black high school. I have memories of the high school I attended, but few of them are positive.

I have always been insulted by the notion that African Americans cannot be properly educated unless whites are in the classroom. I feel that we should have used that energy to demand improved conditions in our own schools and to teach our children pride in their heritage.

It seemed cowardly to me that children were used as the battering ram to desegregate this society, and it didn't work. The social life of children is usually orchestrated by their parents. Many parents, both black and white, picked up their families and moved rather than be involved. Others, myself included, incurred the expense of a private school instead of sacrificing their children to political hardball.

Affirmative action requirements in the workplace have been far more effective than desegregation of schools in bringing people together from various ethnic groups and improving the economic conditions of African Americans. People who work together over a period of time have to depend on each other and learn to know one another as individuals, not as representatives of an ethnic group.

*And Justice for All*

The United States . . . becomes the world's most interesting laboratory for working out the intricate issues of race adjustment.

**Kelly Miller**

When it comes to the cause of justice, I take no prisoners and I don't believe in compromising.

**Mary Frances Berry**

In an effort to make one unified nation out of this country during its formative period, much emphasis was placed on eradicating national differences and boundaries and making a "melting pot" of "Americans" out of individuals from various immigrant groups. Biological interaction, as well as certain activities, were encouraged among certain ethnic groups to facilitate the melting. For other designated groups (depending on who was calling the shots, and when) melting was prohibited.

Notwithstanding the many past and contemporary mistakes that have been committed, the United States of America still has the opportunity to achieve harmony among a collection of people from all over the world. Instead of insisting upon the dominance of a particular group, we can do the unprecedented and actually get along with each other despite our differences. Even though we represent the ultimate in repudiated groups, African Americans are largely responsible for making this rapprochement possible by insisting that the country live up to its expressed ideals.

### My Mother

My mother's love had been imperfect but everlasting.

**Marita Golden in *Migrations of the Heart***

I had a great mother. She didn't have much power, but she did all she could for me.

**Louis Armstrong**

I didn't realize how close my mother and I were until after she had died. Then I discovered, from swapping stories with my siblings, that she had shared many things with me that she never told them. When I was growing up, she was very supportive of my aspirations. (I know now that my dreams mirrored her own.) Our basic personalities, however, were different, possibly as a result of her not having grown up with a loving mother; her own mother died when she was six years old.

Mama was a pessimist and I have always been relentlessly optimistic, so we clashed many times. Against her wishes and with my ears and heart full with her fears, I moved away from my hometown and became ever more adventurous.

Golden's and Armstrong's statements could both be said about my mother. Although I chafed under her constant admonitions not to overreach myself, one thing I never doubted was her everlasting love.

She will always be with me.

# Racism

It is critical that we take charge of our own destiny and stop waiting for some unknown mythical being to come along and wipe racism from the face of this earth.

**David C. Wilson**

Let [racism] be a problem to someone else . . . Let it drag them down. Don't use it as an excuse for your own shortcomings.

**Colin Powell**

Racism is a power play; it is used to control people's behavior. Some people act as racists to prevent those who look different from participating in some activity. Other people, especially politicians, use the presence of racism to divide people, to provoke guilt, or so they can be viewed as victims. Most people find that it feels better to blame someone else for shortcomings than to take responsibility for improving their behavior; and it's certainly easier.

Making scapegoats of people we don't like or understand is apparently a human quality that is not only common, but to be expected. Fights between groups, states, and nations are as old as humanity and as current as Bosnia and Rwanda. Anthropologists call the belief that your ethnic group is the center of the universe "ethnocentrism." It has also been called "nationalism," "tribalism," and "religious intolerance."

The United States is a country where people have the opportunity to actually get up close and personal not only with those from other cultures, but also with people who look totally different.

We can take charge of our own destiny and benefit from that opportunity, or let racism drag us down. The choice is ours.

## *Villains or Heroes?*

Race is the galvanizing force in many of the so-called hot-button issues of the day: crime, prisons, gun control, welfare reform, affirmative action and immigration. And African Americans are disproportionately represented in the role of social villain.

**Salim Muwakkil**

Would America have been America without her Negro people?

**W.E.B. Du Bois**

Too many politicians are working hard to outdo each other in appealing to racism in the United States with "hot-button issues." The media cooperates by putting a black face on crime and welfare recipients. With blacks and Hispanic immigrants being blamed as the major cause of social problems, alienated whites, who are ignored, have been free to organize and plan terrorist activities.

Women across the country are grateful to Anita Hill and the Clarence Thomas hearings for calling attention to sexual harassment. O. J. Simpson's brutal treatment of his former wife, Nicole, has placed media focus on one of the most shameful behaviors tolerated in this country: violence against women in domestic situations. However, in both situations, the villain's face is, again, black.

Yet, despite the efforts of shameless politicians and thoughtless journalists to divide the country along racial lines, a popular magazine did an admittedly unscientific survey indicating that most women in this country want to be Oprah; most men wish they could be like Mike (Jordan, that is) and Bill Cosby is everybody's favorite person.

No, without us this couldn't be America.

## Music in the Air

Man, I sure had a ball growing up in New Orleans as a kid.
We were poor and everything like that, but music was all around
you. Music kept you rolling.

**Louis Armstrong**

I didn't have much to say about it. It had to be. I didn't choose
music. Music chose me.

**Marian Anderson**

One of the most joyful things about being a person of African
descent is the central place music occupies in our lives.

Like Armstrong's, growing up, my family was "poor and
everything like that," but there was music everywhere. We had a
record player and a piano in our house. Both my sister and I
were given piano lessons, but she, being more talented then I,
had the responsibility of playing for family songfests.

We heard a lot of our music in church, and church hymns
and gospel music remain among my favorites. At one point or
another, everybody in the family sang in one of the church
choirs, and my sister became quite an accomplished church
organist.

Because everybody I knew played music in their homes and at
their parties, I assumed this was universal human behavior. I
was astonished to learn that people (particularly adults) from
other cultures actually had parties without music.

When I traveled to Nigeria several years ago, there were many
events that caused me to have a flash of recognition, but none
more so than attending adult parties where the music was loud
and people were dancing.

### Psychological Warfare

Racism is in large measure a form of psychological warfare.

**Johnnetta Cole in *Conversations***

If you live in an oppressive society, you've got to be very resilient. You can't let each little thing crush you. You have to take every encounter and make yourself larger, rather than allow yourself to be diminished by it.

**James Earl Jones**

A people that has been conquered, enslaved, colonized, oppressed, and discriminated against has only two options— fight back or submit. Submitting is easier; it requires little effort and less thought. You just do as you're told and hope to avoid trouble.

Fighting back is much more difficult. Even when you know you're not going to comply, you still must decide how to fight back. You can go the slash and destroy route, taking down every person or obstacle in your path. Another approach is the one recommended by the grandfather in Ralph Ellison's *Invisible Man:* "Live with your head in the lion's mouth . . . overcome 'em with yeses, undermine 'em with grins, agree 'em to death and destruction, let 'em swoller you till they vomit or bust wide open."

I like Jones's recommendation. I prefer to live my life to the fullest with the resiliency to "take every encounter and make [my]self larger." And better. If I had not run into a "glass ceiling" in the corporate world, I might still be there doing work that made me miserable, rather than here doing what I love most: writing.

# Being Black Is Worth Its Weight

I would not exchange my color for all the wealth in the world, for had I been born white, I might not have been able to do all I have done.

**Mary McLeod Bethune**

The fact is that American whites, as a whole, are just as much in doubt about their nationality, their cultural identity, as are [American blacks].

**Harold Cruse in *The Crisis of the Negro Intellectual***

One of my white friends confessed to me that she envied African Americans their belonging to a specific culture. She is one of the "white bread" European Americans without any ethnic or cultural distinction. Although she is a member of the white upper middle class, her material security cannot replace that sense of belonging to an identifiable group. I can understand her feeling of loss, because I know that for me, being an African American has been more of a blessing than a problem.

Yes, I have been the object of racism and sexism, just like most women of African descent in this country, but I also have a wonderful life. I don't believe there is anything like the triumphant experience of rising above the forces of oppression.

I have lived long enough to learn that how people respond to the color of my skin is far less important than how I feel about myself. Like Bethune, I wouldn't trade being black for anything.

***Are You Black Enough?***

Because I want every kid to be viewed as a person rather than as a member of a certain race does not mean that I'm not black enough.

**Michael Jordan**

Color is not a human or a personal reality; it is a political reality.

**James Baldwin in *The Fire Next Time***

Many African Americans, feeling that institutional and individual racism by Euro-Americans was not cruel enough, decided to refine that practice by creating additional arbitrary and variously defined criteria to measure "blackness."

I admit that during the volatile sixties, I, too, was caught up in "how black" particular folks were, until I discovered that by somebody else's yardstick, even I was not considered "truly" black. According to some standards, *really black* black people have no interest in certain recreational activities, in careers in specific fields, or in having noncompulsory contact with whites. My son and nephews also discovered that being an honor student in some schools was definitely a "white thing."

Fabricating a pattern into which all members of an ethnic group must fit is oppressive no matter who does it. In *Fatheralong*, John Edgar Wideman says that "Race preempts our right to situate our story where we choose. It casts us as minor characters in somebody else's self-elevating melodrama." I have determined where my individual human life will be located, and neither white racism or barometers of blackness will have a material impact on my personal decision.

## My African Heritage

The cruelest thing slavery and colonialism did to the Africans was to destroy their memory of what they were before foreign contact.

**John Henrik Clarke**

I must see [Africa], get close to it, because I can never lose the sense of being a displaced person here in America because of my color.

**Paule Marshall**

In this country, African Americans are taught that their history began with slavery and ends with racial prejudice and economic problems. Traditionally there has been nothing included in school textbooks to make us proud. This is, of course, by design, to make us feel inferior and ashamed of who we are. My parents taught us to take pride in ourselves, but they knew nothing of our history before slavery and sharecropping, and they didn't care to discuss that. We looked forward because there was nothing good in looking back.

When I became aware of my true ancestral roots before slavery, I wanted to see Africa for myself. I'm glad I did, because that first trip totally eradicated the savage-jungle image I had grown up with. Many African Americans have no interest in Africa. Some deny that Africa has anything to do with who we are, but for me, knowing as much about Africa as I can strengthens me, and I intend to keep going back.

## Wells of Spiritual Strength

I
am Today's Woman. Today's Woman
is not ward nor toy nor curio nor game,
nor slavey in this sun-time of the monsters.

**Gwendolyn Brooks in *Winnie***

The black woman has deep wells of spiritual strength.

**Margaret Walker Alexander**

Until I left a secure job and struck out on my own, I had no idea what spiritual strength I was heir to. I couldn't have picked a worse time to make such a move: I was the single parent of an 11-year-old child; my father, who had been one of the pillars holding me up, was dead; and my mother, the other pillar, was critically ill.

I increased my stress level by selling my home and moving halfway across the country to a city where I knew no one, but which was close to home, family, and Mama. I really had no idea what I was doing, except that it was absolutely essential for me to make a substantive change in my life.

My decision led to ten of the toughest years of my life. But I also learned how strong I am and what I am capable of accomplishing. Since my mother's death, there are times when I feel utterly alone, but these are also the times when I drink deeply from my well of spiritual strength.

I am today's woman.

### Still Learning

The specialism and visible success of the sciences have impressed some minds to such a degree that they have virtually identified the possibilities of human knowledge with the possibilities of science.

**W. E. Abraham in *The Mind of Africa***

I grew up in a religious home with parents who believed in God and a mother who occasionally had prophetic dreams. Spirituality was a reality in our home. However, my parents also believed in the power of knowledge and education, so when my teachers and professors instructed me that nothing is factual if it cannot be proven scientifically, I briefly became agnostic.

My spiritual base was too firm for me to be rid of it so easily, so I began to study other cultures and non-Christian religions. What I learned is that humans throughout time and all over the world are far more alike than they are different. I can't believe that this similarity in human development is a result of random occurrences.

From my own experiential knowledge and from what I've read, I am absolutely certain that there is a superintelligence (God, Jehovah, Allah) as well as an order in the universe that applies to all of life, including humans. I am equally sure that the most important aspects of this world are unquantifiable by current scientific methods.

I believe that we haven't yet closed in on the possibilities of human knowledge and that the scientific world, like me, has much to learn.

# Creating My Own Reality

If anybody's going to help African American people, it's got to be ourselves.

**Earvin "Magic" Johnson**

It matters less what you acquire than what you endure to acquire it. . . . Waste no tears on me. I didn't come along too early— I was right on time.

**John Jordan "Buck" O'Neil, Jr.**

Several years ago I purchased a small pamphlet because it promised to instruct me on how to get along with difficult people. I was quite astonished to read that the first thing I needed to do was to treat the "difficult" person with honesty and love. The pamphlet also said that I should stop expecting other people to be difficult, and that the best way to have a happy life was to be happy myself.

I was so surprised at this unexpected directive that I decided to try it. First, I decided to find things in my life to be happy about, which caused me to remember my mother's repeatedly telling us to count our blessings. Then I made a conscious effort to smile at everybody. From there I began to look for something good in everybody with whom I had an encounter. I began to feel better, happier; most amazingly, the people I had thought were difficult either drifted out of my life, or I no longer felt bothered by them.

Now I pay attention to happy people like Magic Johnson and Buck O'Neil. They bring a positive spirit to their experiences; consequently, no matter what happens in their lives—HIV, playing in a segregated baseball league—they continue to beam. It works for me too.

## Being Childish

As children we begin our journey of acceptance and approval. We open our hearts freely trusting the goodness of others—until a person or event rejects that which is lovingly given . . . We stop trusting. Eventually we must go inside; we experience the Death, Burial, and Resurrection of our Spirit or nature. We experience a transformation.

**Shirley Jo Finney**

I know this transformation. I'm experiencing it. A large part of knowing that I am on the right path, again, has been the resurrection of my childhood thoughts.

Children are naturally loving and spontaneous, open, honest about their feelings, nonjudgmental. They trust that they will be cared for, accepted for themselves. We've all been there, although our memory of it may be overlaid with deep layers of negative trauma.

Returning to that ability to be childlike is arduous, but it's also an adventure that is well worth the effort. The real beauty of this search for my essential self is that I can change. No matter how many mistakes I've made in the past, I can let go of the guilt and shame of having done the wrong thing, and be transformed.

# Television and Children

Television provides experiences that many children would not have otherwise.

James P. Comer, M.D., & Alvin F. Poussaint, M.D., in
*Black Child Care*

Many responsible and intelligent people rail against television as the enemy of education, reading, and creative thinking. I don't agree.

I was in high school before Daddy bought a television for our family. I was a bookworm then and remain so today, but I also watch television. My son became interested in television at about age 3 and after that I wasn't able to keep him away from it. His intense interest has continued until the present.

As a small child, he favored children's programs like *Sesame Street, The Electric Company,* and *Mr. Rogers,* but as he grew older, he liked to watch everything. I didn't restrict what he watched, but we often watched together and discussed what we had seen. Even though I failed in getting the television turned off while he did his homework, he remained an excellent student.

He has an equally avid interest in reading. At bedtime, given a choice between television and his nightly story, he never chose television. For both of us, television has exposed us to places, events, scenes, and thoughts that we might otherwise not have experienced.

We already know that when a book is adapted for television or the movies, that book has a huge increase in sales. If I had the power, I would make television an integral part of every classroom, because I believe that could stimulate students' interest in reading and learning.

*Humor*

The comic in this country unites the tragic as well as the mirthful.

**Ralph Ellison**

You all know how black humor started? It started on slave ships. Cat was rowing and dude says, "What you laughin' about?" He said, "Yesterday I was a king."

**Richard Pryor in *Pryor Convictions and Other Life Sentences***

I've always thought that a big laugh is a really loud noise from the soul saying, "Ain't that the truth."

**Quincy Jones**

Leave it to Richard Pryor to identify, with a succinct joke, the ability of African Americans to laugh in the face of disaster. Along with our music, our ability to laugh at ourselves and our predicament has been instrumental in our survival.

Even though I have often taken myself much too seriously, my being able to triumph over the problems of my life is due largely to my willingness to laugh at myself. I also prefer the company of people with whom I can share a hearty laugh, and I make a concerted effort to find something funny whenever I'm feeling depressed or sad.

Finding humor in misfortune not only helps you to cope, but makes you feel better while doing so.

# Doing Your Job Well

If a man is called to be a streetsweeper . . . he should sweep streets so well that all the hosts of heaven and earth will pause to say, here lived a great streetsweeper who did his job well.

**Martin Luther King, Jr.**

One of the most important things our parents taught my siblings and me was to always do a good job, no matter how unpleasant or humble the task. My mother had us memorize the poem "Be the Best of Whatever You Are." My father, whose 4th grade education limited him to manual labor, thought highly of himself and his reputation, so he was always punctual and did every job thoroughly.

Daddy's several part-time "extra" jobs enabled us to own a home and a car, and to take wonderful family vacations. Daddy boasted that he could always find work and that he had a job throughout the Depression.

Daddy obtained his first job after he left the South by repeatedly returning to a construction site near where he lived and asking for work. One day after the site boss had told him yet again that he was not hiring, Daddy picked up a wheelbarrow and started working. Within a couple of hours the astonished site boss offered him a job.

As a result of Mama's encouragement and Daddy's example, I have always been confident about my ability to take care of myself. If Daddy, who was born 38 years after the Civil War and had far less education than I, could always support himself and his family, I knew I would do no less.

I shared Daddy's story with my son, who continues the family tradition of being a conscientious, competent worker.

## Friends as Family

Their friendship was as intense as it was sudden. They found relief
in each other's personality.

**Toni Morrison in** *Sula*

The idea of family is constantly shifting, so varied in its many
shapes that the narrative of family is as unpredictable as
families themselves.

**Mary Helen Washington in** *Memory of Kin*

I am blessed to have several wonderful, supportive friends,
but there are some who are special treasures in my life.

As a single parent I know firsthand how difficult it is to rear a
child without a partner. Children need as many folks as possible
to love and support them. If those loving people are the parents,
grandparents, aunts and uncles, great; but in many cases and for
many reasons, that is not always possible.

My friends and I provided that additional support and love
for our children who were living in single-parent homes. In each
case, our children had contact with their fathers, but the dads
and other relatives lived out of state and could see the children
only during summers and on holidays. So, on a daily and week-
ly basis, my friends and I were the "other parent" for the children. We exchanged weekends of child care, took the others'
children in when our jobs required us to travel, and reinforced
each other's disciplinary practices.

We each had only one child, so the shared responsibilities
also allowed the children to experience "siblings."

I had similar arrangements with friends who were married
couples, so my son had the benefit of male surrogate parents as
well. Consequently, his family circle was wider than those of
many other children, and although we no longer live near these
friends, we still retain our "family" ties.

## Knowing Your Strengths

When you look in the mirror, know who is looking back at you. When you know your strengths and recognize your weaknesses, you can create art.

**Debbie Allen**

One of the most difficult things I've had to learn is that taking care of myself does not mean that I am selfish. I now understand that it is impossible for me to be a wise parent, a good friend, a supportive partner, or to do excellent work, if I don't take care of myself.

Caring for myself means finding time to assess my strengths and weaknesses; to discover the authentic me, rather than the me I think others expect me to be. Taking care of myself means knowing what I want, as well as what I need, to be a healthy, balanced, happy person. I've found the best way to attain this self-knowledge is to periodically remove myself from work, responsibility, and family so that I can relax, reflect, and pamper myself.

When I take care of myself, I am at my best. I am able to be creative or to assist in the care of someone else.

## A Happy Home

A two-parent home is no better off than a single-parent one if the father is fucked up in the head and beaten down. There's nothing more dangerous and destructive in a household than a frustrated, oppressed black man.

### Nathan McCall in *Makes Me Wanna Holler*

Understanding what permits many single mothers to raise successful children may be every bit as important as understanding the power of paternal love.

### Ellis Cose

I wasted a lot of energy feeling guilty because my son's father and I were not rearing our child together, and being embarrassed that I was a contributor to the endless number of "broken" homes.

My attitude began to change at a family gathering when my sister pointed out that, although I was the only single parent among our siblings (at that time), my child was as well behaved and happy as any of his cousins. My sister's observation brought to mind my son's 1st-grade teacher, who had been astonished that a child whom she considered exceptionally well adjusted did not live with both parents.

I made a decision that my life and my child's life would improve if he lived with one happy parent rather than with two unhappy ones. I do not regret that decision. At 22 he is still a happy, well-adjusted person, and so am I.

## Defining Ourselves

If I didn't define myself for myself, I would be crunched into other people's fantasies for me and eaten alive.

**Audre Lorde in *Sister Outsider***

A few of my female friends and I are engaging in revolutionary behavior. We tell our ages, are more concerned about our health than our weight, don't dye our hair, and believe the Wonder Bra is a relic of the Dark Ages much like the chastity belt.

My brother sent me a bag full of snapshots taken at family gatherings over the years, and I made an awesome discovery. I was never fat! This may seem like an unimportant piece of information, but I had spent most of my life in agony because my family and my husbands (*after* we were married) said that I was too fat. In some of the pictures, I was downright thin, probably just after one of the many diets I tried.

It has taken years of psychotherapy and spiritual development for me to look at those pictures and be able to see myself as I really was, rather than as I was defined by someone else.

I weigh more than I ever did, except when I was pregnant, but I'm healthier and happier than I thought it was possible to be. My life isn't perfect, but it is *my* life. I've learned that—

*If others' opinions*
*Count too much with me,*
*Then I will become*
*What the opinion of others*
*Say that I should be.*

*Basketball as Metaphor*

The game is scheduled. We have to play it. We might as well win.

**Bill Russell**

You don't have to be an athlete to be a good sport.

**Mildred Morgan Ball**

Basketball games move quickly and require the players' undivided attention. The players who are in top physical and mental condition are able to play the entire game, while others don't get a lot of playing time.

Focus is important. When players are distracted, either by the referees' sometimes patently unfair calls, or the "trash talking" of opposing players, the game continues without them, and the team is seriously disadvantaged. No matter how skilled and talented the superstars may be, they need the entire team to win championships.

Although basketball selects for exceptionally tall, muscular body types, outstanding players come in different shapes and, even with the constant running, some players never become thin. Players like Muggsy Bogues and Spud Webb have demonstrated that even short players can be successful at the game.

As in the rest of life, the people in charge make up new rules with which the players must comply. Complaining about rule changes is a waste of time, but those issues can be raised when new agreements are being negotiated.

We can't control every aspect of our lives, but we can be determined to win at whatever we do. Winning means doing our best and having fun in the process.

## Gratitude for What We Have

If I never play another basketball game, I would be forever grateful for the success I've had in this game. People have to look at things for what they have, not what they haven't been given.

**Hakeem Olajuwon**

Olajuwon made this statement before he and the Houston Rockets won back-to-back National Basketball Association championships. Although I am a serious fan of the Chicago Bulls, watching the Rockets play basketball is a special pleasure.

In particular, Olajuwon's easy grace reminds me of a delightful discovery I made when I visited Nigeria. Nigerians have a pride in themselves that is clearly perceptible, but not exhibitionist. I've rarely seen people like that in the U.S., but I suppose it's not to be expected in a country so young and unsure of itself.

It would be rather difficult to be grateful for what you have without also taking pride in who you are. However, in the U.S., we have billion-dollar industries devoted to making people over. Very few people are either satisfied with the way they look or with what they have, no matter how much it is. There seems no way ever to get enough of anything. Everybody is expected to be trying for a promotion, a better job, more money, more expensive clothing, a bigger house, to expand the business. Being content is out of the question, and we have the stress indicators to prove it.

I'm trying to learn to relax and to be grateful for what I have.

### A Swinging Door

Trying to live without friends is like milking a bear to get cream for your morning coffee. It is a whole lot of trouble, and then not worth much after you get it.

**Zora Neale Hurston in *Dust Tracks on a Road***

To love is to make of one's heart a swinging door.

**Howard Thurman**

The wiser I become, the more I understand that the most valuable treasures in my life are my friends, and I include my adult son in that group. I have deep, powerful feelings for my close friends. I love them.

As a posttherapeutic adult, I have come to understand that human beings can have deeply felt nonerotic love relationships. I was reared in a family where feelings were suppressed and denied; we never saw our parents either argue or hug. Consequently, for many years I either denied the love I felt for my family and friends, both male and female, or endured feelings of shame and guilt. I believed that the only valid relationship involving strong feelings was a prelude to sex.

In my opinion, if this culture was not so mesmerized with sex, and focused more on the characteristics of nonerotic love, our success rate with erotic pairings might improve. We might also have less incest and pedophilia. Sometimes I think that the human fear of unrestrained, unconditional love is the reason why life on this earth sometimes seems like hell. For if we were able to love one another, openly, directly, fully, this would be heaven, wouldn't it?

I'm learning to love my friends unconditionally and without fear of how my love may be interpreted; my life is richer for it.

## The Joy of Learning

What it was that seemed to move me then was that learning was important. I'd never thought that before . . . The employment agency approach of most schools I guess, does not emphasize the beauties the absolute joy of learning.

**Amiri Baraka** in *The Autobiography of*
*Leroi Jones/Amiri Baraka*

I take great joy in learning and have always been an avid reader, but many of my most precious lessons have been outside of school and books. Several years ago, I had a job that required me to work closely with two other women. Because we spent so much time together, we learned to like one another and became friends. One of the reasons I liked each of these women was that they were both as passionate about their ethnic backgrounds as I am about being African American.

Mary is Irish American and Elena is Mexican American. In addition to personal tales, Elena filled me in on the story of her people, none of which had been included in my history textbooks. And Mary pointed out to me that several of my favorite English writers were, in fact, Irish.

Having grown up in a racially segregated environment, I didn't have friends from other ethnic groups during my school years. These two women taught me a lot, not the least of which was that friends can be found anywhere.

## *Money: What's It Worth?*

Violence is a country where property counts more than people.

**Julian Bond**

If [a man] looked prosperous, women would pull him by his dick into the bed and then hit him with a paternity suit nine months later. If a woman had money, the man would just beat her until she got up off of it.

**Walter Mosley in *Black Betty***

Money is meant to be spent, or saved; whichever makes you feel good. My mother taught us that if we made a quarter, we should save a nickel. Mama believed in having money in the bank, in saving for a "rainy day." I was an obedient child far into my adult life. I always had money in the bank. I deprived myself of things that I wanted in order to save the requisite amount every month. Sometimes I said I was broke (and truly felt that way) because the only money I had was the thousands in savings and investments.

All of that changed when I decided that I wanted to enjoy my life every minute of every day. No longer do I save for some unforeseeable future; my future is now. If I want something that requires money, I purchase it. My change in behavior was triggered by observing Mama's last years. She refused to buy anything except absolute necessities and didn't perceive anything as being so essential that she should take money out of the bank. Her "rainy day" never came.

I know many people whose sense of security is inseparable from their net worth, and I understand that, having been there. However, I've learned to derive a sense of well-being from a higher power than my material holdings.

## Measuring Up

Data [for blacks] is most often used to tell a story of continuing inequities . . . This is certainly not untrue, but the danger of such an emphasis is that it too often only serves to reinforce a collective sense of inferiority by suggesting that blacks never quite measure up.

**Audrey Edwards and Craig K. Polite in**
*Children of the Dream*

One of the reasons I decided to send my son to a private school was so that he would learn how to do well on standardized tests. For those of us who don't have money and/or powerful connections, standardized tests are used to decide the parameters of our future.

I recall that I didn't learn the technique of test-taking in the segregated elementary school I attended. Consequently, as a result of my scores on the placement test for high school I was assigned to an English class for retarded students (now called special education). At the desegregated high school I was encouraged to major in home economics so that I would learn to be a good domestic worker.

My educational experience is not at all unusual, especially for black students, and any student whose parents are uninformed can be shafted by these exams. Standardized tests are used not to find out what students are capable of doing, but rather to keep certain people away from specific opportunities. What better way to do this than with a "standardized, objective" test that reveals that those people don't measure up.

We have to move beyond systems that are designed to limit us to develop our own programs that encourage our growth.

## *Values and Politics*

Dissension is healthy, even when it gets loud.

Jennifer Lawson

No amount of persuasion can change a man's reaction to what he knows. But what he knows can be changed.

**Dennis Kimbro and Napoleon Hill** in
*Think and Grow Rich: A Black Choice*

There appears to be a popular consensus in the country that our values have eroded, that in some previous halcyon time, we had universal high moral standards.

People behave the same way we always have: We are vicious, unselfish, violent, caring, greedy, loving, and narrow-minded. We are good, and we lie, cheat, and steal. What has changed is our communications technology. Acts that were once hidden away and kept secret can now be seen daily, live and in living color on television.

Most of the talk about "values" seems to focus on the behavior of young people: teenage mothers, rap music, gangs, and so on. Of course, we should encourage and celebrate the best behavior in everyone, but rather than berating those whose behavior we find distasteful, why not set an example of loving, caring self-respect for them to emulate?

When those who lament our fallen standards begin to focus on the behavior of the power brokers and our elected leaders, rather than the powerless, I will be more inclined to believe that they are serious and not just playing politics.

Most people's behavior is shaped by what they know. We can't have a society that treats great numbers of people as if they were disposable and then expect those same people to be purveyors of good works.

## Transformation

My message now is calmer, forever seeking the transformation and reconciliation that come from hope, love and forgiveness.

**Barbara Reynolds**

At one point, I would have to say that I was a "hothead," with rigid ideas about some of the things I believed in. After spending time reflecting on my life and examining my behavior, I figured out that there were many things about me that could use some improvement. It has been a painful process, but I am now able to look at myself honestly and see my flaws as well as my strengths.

I can see that many of my problems are self-generated. Seeing myself as I am has also made it easier for me to accept imperfection in others. Because I want people to forgive me my mistakes, I am willing to suspend judgment of theirs. The power to change, to learn and to grow, to transform yourself, is what makes this life worthwhile.

## Victory of the Spirit

I must oppose any attempt that Negroes may make to do to others what has been done to them . . . I know the spiritual wasteland to which that road leads . . . whoever debases others is debasing himself.

**James Baldwin in The Fire Next Time**

Out of the heart are the issues of life and no external force, however great and overwhelming, can at long last destroy a people if it does not first win the victory of the spirit against them.

**Howard Thurman in Jesus and the Disinherited.**

It is difficult in the extreme to have pride and self-respect when those in authority, including elected and appointed government officials, use their several advantages to demonstrate that African Americans have no rights they are bound to respect—that, in fact, our presence in "their country" is for their ease and convenience: to do the hard, dirty work they find distasteful, or to entertain them in a manner they determine.

However, no matter how difficult it is, we must not allow ourselves to be defined by laws, traditions, and institutions that were developed to humiliate and destroy us. The fact that we have not been obliterated, despite their best efforts, is a tribute to the persuasive spiritual power of African people. We have not only refused to succumb to the terrorism, but our courage has served as a model for other oppressed people in this country and around the world.

*A luta continua,* the struggle continues, and African Americans will thrive so long as we retain our spiritual ascendancy.

# Index

## About the Author

JANET CHEATHAM BELL has been a librarian, an educator, and an editor. Currently she is experiencing her lifelong dream of being a full-time writer. She lives in Chicago, her favorite city, where she has a spectacular view of Lake Michigan that she says is essential to her spiritual tranquility.